The Money Doctor's Guide to Taking Care of Yourself When No One Else Will

The Money Doctor's Guide to Taking Care of Yourself When No One Else Will

W. NEIL GALLAGHER, PhD

WILEY

John Wiley & Sons, Inc.

Published by John Wiley & Sons, Inc., Hoboken, New Jersey.
Published simultaneously in Canada.

For general information on our other products and services or for technical support, please contact our Customer Care Department within the United States at (800) 762-2974, outside the United States at (317) 572-3993 or fax (317) 572-4002.

Wiley also publishes its books in a variety of electronic formats. Some content that appears in print may not be available in electronic books. For more information about Wiley products, visit our web site at www.wiley.com.

Designations used by companies to distinguish their products are often claimed by trademarks. In all instances where the author or the publisher is aware of a claim, the product names appear in Initial Capital letters. Readers, however, should contact the appropriate companies for more complete information regarding trademarks and registration.

Medicaid rules are subject to change. Information in Chapter 5 is a description of Medicaid rules as we understand them at the time of publication. Nothing in Chapter 5 is to be interpreted as an attempt to defraud the government in order to qualify for Medicaid. To the contrary, we militate against such a strategy. We urge the reader to provide for his or her own health and financial resources.

Library of Congress Cataloging-in-Publication Data:

Gallagher, W. Neil, 1941–
    The money doctor's guide to taking care of yourself when no one else will / W. Neil Gallagher.
      p. cm.
    Includes bibliographical references.
    ISBN-13: 978-0-471-69744-2 (pbk.)
    ISBN-10: 0-471-69744-3 (pbk.)
    1. Older people—United States—Finance, Personal. 2. Middle aged persons—United States—Finance, Personal. 3. Estate planning—United States. 4. Older people—Long-term care—United States. 5. Insurance, Long-term care—United States. 6. Medicare. 7. Nursing homes—United States. 8. Retirement—United States. I. Title.
HG179.G2645 2006
332.024'0084'6—dc22

                        2005018424

Printed in the United States of America.

10 9 8 7 6 5 4 3 2 1

Your Greatest Fear

Chronic, long-term disabilities threaten the health and welfare of many. . . . The number of older citizens needing long-term care is expected to increase by 70 percent over the next 50 years. I urge all . . . to plan ahead to meet their long-term care needs, including ways to finance their long-term care expenses.

—George W. Bush

The Dos

I *do* want my time of passing to be free of regrets and full of tranquility.

I *do* want to die at home, pain free, in my own bed, and with my loved ones around me—when the time comes.

I *do* agree with this statement:

I want to control my person and property while I am alive and well. I want to provide for myself and my loved ones AT ALL TIMES and, in my final days, give what I own to whom I want, the way I want, and when I want, and save every last tax dollar, attorney fee, and court cost possible. If healthcare decisions are made for me by another, I want to appoint—ahead of time—the person who makes those decisions, and give him or her clear directions on my healthcare choices.

The Don'ts

I *don't* want to spend my final days in a nursing home.

I *don't* want to be on welfare (Medicaid).

I *don't* want my family's health and finances ravaged because of my aging and death.

If you disagree with these three statements, slam the book shut.

Contents

Preface

To my fellow baby-boomers:

You are taking care of a parent, spouse, or other loved one right now. . . . Good for you! You recognize that life is intrinsically valuable. You are tapping into, and dramatizing, our rich Judeo-Christian heritage, which recognizes that life is sacred, special, and valuable from conception to death, from womb to grave, and from infant cradle to hospital bed.

Because of your unconditional love for that sacred and special life, it doesn't matter how foul your loved one smells, how expensive it is to take care of him or her, or how cantankerous he or she becomes. You're taking care of your loved one unconditionally and sacrificially because, made in the image of God, he or she is beautiful.

And so are you.

My prayer is that this book empowers you to take even better care of your loved ones—and yourself.

Your Friend,
"Doc" Gallagher

INTRODUCTION

From Welfare to Wealth: My Story

I DON'T KNOW WHY HE WAS SICK ALL THE TIME. NO ONE ELSE'S FATHER was. He was always coughing, wheezing, choking, in comas, and in and out of hospitals. When would he get well? When would we be a normal family? I guess never.

His TB put us on welfare and landed him in that infamous Boston sanatorium, miles down the road from our home in Lawrence, the "armpit of the east," memorialized in Alan Farnham's book:

> There were no "Café Budapests" in Lawrence . . . the section where mills were located was considered by locals to be among the city's toughest, a wasteland of shuttered shops and broken windows. . . .
>
> Life for working men and women in Lawrence had never been easy (the city was the scene for 1912's Bread and Roses strike by 25,000 workers), but at least the city had once bustled with commercial activity. Now, it ranked twenty-fourth among the poorest cities in the United States, no longer famous for manufacturing, but for being a crack-cocaine capital

1

and a magnet for newly arrived immigrants. Though only 30 miles north of Boston, it might as well have been in the third world.[1]

And in our patch of the third world (our tenement of broken windows crushed between shuttered shops across from the mills) things never got better, only worse . . . and only to *us*. That's how it looked to a hungry thirteen-year-old, clothed in Salvation Army discards, crouched in an icy corner room in December.

Suicide seemed an attractive option.

Why not? At least I wouldn't have to look at those guys anymore: Charlie Grady, Eddie Wacker, or Lennie Gaboury. They lived in matchbox tenements like we did, but the rest was different.

They had cars. They had refrigerators. They had heat in the winter. They had paychecks coming in each week.

They never had their lights and heat shut off. They never were evicted in the chill of winter. They never were denied food. (As many times as it happens, you never get used to having a glass of water for breakfast . . . and lunch . . . and supper.)

They didn't hear dishes—pitched at a drunken father—smash against kitchen walls. They didn't hear a mother wail and scream, watching beer destroy a sick man whose lust for beer kept food from the mouths of two sons.

Because of his drinking, poor eating, and failing to take adequate insulin, he slipped in and out of consciousness. Morning after morning, we poured orange juice and sugared water down his gurgling, resisting throat.

When I was fifteen, I watched him die in my mother's lap. Frantically, she rubbed her hands up and down his back, back and forth across his chest, trying to revive him—to no avail. She rained tears on his motionless body, looking like Mary in the *Pietà*, in agony over a limp, cold form. He died quickly. Her fierce loyalty had kept him alive for many years. Now, it was over.

His death occurred during a rare happy moment in their lives. Following three months of separation, they had decided to try it again. They were determined to stop screaming and cursing. They were determined to love . . . again.

He was not going to drink. He was going to take his medicine regularly.

They were reunited only a few weeks—no drunken fights, no comas. He really took care of himself. That Sunday afternoon, they took a quick nap. His self-injected insulin shot wasn't due for a couple of hours—no problem.

But they overslept. She woke up and found him swooning off in a coma. She administered orange juice—sugared water. He coughed, gurgled, and swallowed—looked routine. We waited— no response. She tried more orange juice, more sugared water; it was too late. The doctor later said his heart simply could stand no more comas.

Others dictated funeral and burial arrangements. Welfare's lousy for handling death. We had no choice. We had no money and no insurance. I didn't understand it.

Mother went back to work for $40 a week and we still couldn't afford our holes-in-the-wall and rats-in-the-closet tenement. I looked for full-time work, but she insisted I stay in school. When I finished high school, she urged me to attend college. I worked 40 hours a week at night, and earned a degree during the day, be- coming the first one in my family to do so.

After graduation, I joined the Peace Corps and lived on survival wages. I lived on $50 a month (made $75 and sent $25 home), nursing and teaching in leper colonies in northern Thailand.

Two years later, I returned to the States.

After marriage and entrance to graduate school, my wife and I, during a seven-year stretch, raised two toddlers, worked on two M.A.s and a Ph.D., and lived on $62.34 a week.

We made it, thanks in part to welfare's lessons of living on crumbs. Welfare's lessons are enduring and hard. You remember welfare a long time because it humiliates and degrades. You feel shame. You feel you're a victim.

You feel you have to say, "Yes, Sir" and shut up. You feel you have to apologize for everything you want. And your sense of weakness ignites resentment. You develop a slave mentality.

You don't go to the supermarket or toy store. (What are they?) You don't have a doctor. You have no money for meds. Any health care you receive is doled out as charity, at their convenience, after waiting in l-o-n-g lines.

But the wait gives you time to think, What good is coming out of this? Welfare teaches you that a negative attitude is torture; impulsive buying is suicide; and lack of planning is lack of love for yourself and the ones you love. Welfare gives you a fearful respect for money, one that lingers long after you dump welfare.

My goal now is to help others take responsibility for their money and health decisions. For the past 20 years, my life's focus, passion, and crusade has been to help others to retire "Safe, Early and Happy!" In short, my goal is to help others be accountable for their health and financial future.

This is available to everyone in America.

I proved it.

Told you I went to Thailand as one of the first Peace Corps volunteers. We responded to President John F. Kennedy's call: "Ask not what your country can do for you; ask what you can do for your country!"

I fed and nursed lepers with no toes, no eyes, and no nose. Strips of cloth stuck to body parts for years. The smell made you want to wretch. . . . Yet I loved caring for them. I gave them my clothes and my food until I ran out.

What an opportunity for unconditional love and creative action! (There was nothing the lepers could give back in return.)

What an opportunity to rise above the welfare mentality of "give up and shut up"!

They needed someone who wouldn't give up and wouldn't shut up. They needed a passionate advocate who would clean their sores, feed their tissue-thin muscles, and champion their cause.

I took them to hospitals in Chiengmai and Bangkok for meds and surgery to relieve the ravages of the disease. I found clean homes for their children, safe havens free of leprosy, homes that nourished them until they could be reunited with their disease-free parents!

My life with lepers taught me that the poorest welfare bums among us (like the Gallaghers) were Donald-Trump rich compared to most of the world.

After the Peace Corps, I hitchhiked around the world—Berlin, Belfast, Baguio City. Everywhere I went, people flocked to me (Old Glory was sewn on my backpack).

"Can you help me get to America?" they asked me.

America . . . where you can work as hard as you want, as long as you want, in any profession you want. Where you can work, speak, play, worship, and vote freely.

I wanted my leprosy friends free of disease. And today, I want my American friends free of another disease: the disease of G-S-P.

G	overnment is good.
S	ociety is bad.
P	eople are helpless.

GSP is silent and systemic, contagious and fatal. With GSP, you give up. You see everyone else giving up. You have no control over your future (so you think). You surrender life and death, health and family to government.

You make no preparations to retire. You accept Social Security as your sole financial source for retirement—a dangerous retreat.[2] You make no preparations for aging and illness. You accept welfare (Medicaid) as your ultimate health plan.

You choose to surrender your freedom. This is dangerous, humiliating, and unnecessary. This book rescues you from that danger and restores your freedom, leaving you free to *choose* in health or sickness, play or work, aging or dying.

Curious.

Big Ivy League U scoffed at those freedoms. My classes in philosophy, economics, psychology, and political science were brainwashing drills: "Government is good; society is bad; people are helpless."

I got my Ph.D. and left the university scene to become a stockbroker.

I discovered that Big Broker in New York City didn't care much about these freedoms either (neither did Big Broker in St. Louis for whom I later worked). All Big Broker wanted me to do was sell, sell, sell *their stocks/bonds, mutual funds, CDs, annuities, insurance, and real estate.*

Freedom requires education and I educated clients, but Big Broker didn't want me to educate, telling me, flat out: "Doc, don't spend so much time teaching these people. They'll figure out that they can do a lot of this stuff themselves or they'll just go to someone closer to where they live."

I bolted.

I dumped Big Broker and developed my own company dedicated to educating, empowering, and encouraging clients.

I am here to tell you that you *can* retire safe, early, and *happy and healthy.* Your final years need not be years of pain and panic.

Dave Pelzer in *Help Yourself*[3] stated the problem well:

I strongly believe that as a society, we sometime ago crossed a threshold in which a great number of individuals today give up on themselves too easily. We have raised a generation who not only looks for others to rescue them in virtually every matter concerning their lives, but one that also demands that others—whether parents, friends, employees, or the government—immediately solve their problems to their liking.

I learned as a child shivering in my mother's garage the value of personal responsibility and opportunity. Where else but America could I be fortunate enough to turn my life around and, more importantly, provide my son with a chance of living a productive and fulfilling life.

Indeed—where else?

CHAPTER 1

The Pain and the Plea: Nursing Home Abuse[1]

Aging does not bother me a lot; what I worry about is a nursing home.
— A client

My long-term care policy is my letter to my kids. It says to them, "Don't worry about Mom or me going to a nursing home."
— A client

MRS. BRIDGES, AGE 78, WAS A FRIEND FROM CHURCH. MY WIFE AND I VISited her at home weekly. When she went into a nursing home, we continued our weekly visits. Did she need the nursing home? I don't know. It seemed like she was alert and active. Sure, she was a little feeble, beginning to be a little forgetful, but a nursing home?

Every Sunday, my wife and I visited. We noticed the nursing home was old, steamy, and crowded, but what did we know? What could we do? We were not family and had no clout and no experience with nursing homes.

We were her only visitors. Her son never came.

One Saturday, they called and told us Mrs. Bridges was dead. The exam showed that she had died of uremic poisoning. On Tuesday, she had stopped voiding. No one in this nursing home followed up.

Nursing homes deny this, but some patients get no attention . . . unless family's around. It's a tough job: one RN supervising the care of dozens of patients. Most of the nursing assistants work for minimum wage, doing the tough job of patient care day in and day out.

How did this become a national problem, exposing millions of elderly patients like Mrs. Bridges to fear, danger, and humiliation? How were her *most basic* rights trashed?

And how do *you* prevent it from happening to you or your family?

For starters, know your Patients Bill of Rights.

The Patients Bill of Rights

➤ The right to be kept clean and safe.
➤ The right to be informed of your rights and the policies of the home.
➤ The right to be informed about your medical condition and treatment.
➤ The right to choose your own physician.
➤ The right to privacy, dignity, and respect.
➤ The right to be free from abuse and restraints.
➤ The right to be discharged or transferred only for medical reasons.
➤ The right to be informed about the facility's services and charges.
➤ The right to participate in planning your care and medical treatment.
➤ The right to manage personal finances.
➤ The right to personal possessions.
➤ The right to voice grievances without retaliation.
➤ The right to free access.

Apparently, these rights are flagrantly violated with many patients, igniting rage and fear in many, including callers to my radio show:

> Dr. Gallagher, my wife's mom is living with us—has been since my father-in-law died. We love her. . . . She's got Alzheimer's—we think it's Alzheimer's—some kind of dementia. Half the time she doesn't recognize me. Half the time she thinks my wife [her daughter] is her mother. . . . Can we get her some type of care—the care she needs in a good place? We are afraid of a nursing home.   —Brian C.[2]

> Dr. Gallagher, I'm 86 and I'm taking care of my wife, and I'll do that as long as I can. She has to stay in bed pretty much most of the time. I can't get any help. . . . We did pretty well when the stock market was going good. That's how we got the $2½ million. . . . I don't think it will be enough. We both wanted to leave some of that to our kids and some of that to our grandkids and some of it to the church. . . . I don't know how much longer I can continue to take care of her myself. I know one thing: I'll never send her to a nursing home. . . .   —Elmer S.

> Doc, let me tell you about nursing homes. I went through this about fourteen years ago with my parents, and the nursing homes were bloodsuckers. They cost $3,000–$5,000 a month until they ate up all of what my parents had worked all their lives to get. . . . When they charge $3,000–$5,000 for a bed in a 12 × 14 room and they take care of them with unskilled, minimum wage people—that's an inequity. . . . The fault that I find is that there's a disparity imposed for services rendered.   —Victor Z.

My callers, individually and collectively, echo a common fear of isolation, abandonment, neglect, and harm. They are simply terrified of three words: *nursing home abuse.*

In my practice several callers and clients described the most outrageous examples of these. The following are transcript excerpts from callers to my radio show. All names of institutions and individuals have been changed. Let's start with Laura. Her mother went through four nursing homes before landing in one that provided adequate care.

> Doc, when I was in last week to do my rollover, I forgot to tell you about my experiences with long-term care and nursing homes. . . . My mother was practically tortured and about died several times. . . . The care was pitiful. . . . My mother's heel was supposed to be elevated off the bed. It was lying in the bed all the time. . . . Brookside's therapy was really bad. They let my mother's leg freeze up. Yes, my mother's leg is crooked.

That's Laura's story. Dedra called my show the following week and shared some insights into the state of nursing homes today, from the standpoint of a care provider:

> I wanted to shed some light on some of the things you were saying about nursing home care . . . because I've been on the other side of the table. . . . I was once an aide. . . . At the nursing homes that I worked at, we did everything we could to keep the patients hydrated. . . . I'll tell you one thing, too. Not all of us have the attitude that, "Old so-and-so asked for water." . . . We do as much as we possibly can with what little staffing we have. . . . It was so frustrating because . . . we're working under pressure trying not to get written up by the state because we're understaffed, or we're

undersupplied, so on and so forth. It's a much harder job than people make it out to be.

I have one more story to share with you. The story is from a client, Sarah Lomis, who urged me to tell her story after learning I was doing this book.

Dr. Gallagher,

Last week, I dropped in at Fairview Rest Center after a frantic day meeting my deadlines as a paralegal to see my father, Mory, who had been in the center for about a year because of a stroke. . . . I remember vividly that particular day. . . . Dad turned his head away and said softly, "I'm sorry I'm a mess. I put my light on. I tried to call and tell them I had to go to the bathroom. No one came. I'm so miserable."

I stormed down the hall, grabbed the first aide, and screamed loud enough to be heard at the other end of the hall. "Why can't you take care of my father? . . . Isn't that what all that money I pay is supposed to be for? How many times must I come in to find him wet and dirty?" . . . The head nurse told me that an aide was just going into my father's room then. The nurse also informed me that two aides had called in sick that day, and no one could be found to replace them. "Well, that's not my problem!" I screamed at them, louder yet. . . . "My father is sick, and I'm sick and tired of all your excuses."

Doc, my father got cleaned up . . . but imagine what shape he would have been in if I had not stopped in. What about the other residents?

Are these reports of neglect rare and random? According to abundant news reports and in-depth congressional findings, they're not. In fact, an August 2004 news release by *ABC News* found that one in three nursing homes are guilty of elderly abuse, according to a congressional report.

The study, prepared by the minority (Democratic and Independent) staff of the Special Investigations Division of the House Government Reform Committee, found that 30 percent of nursing homes in the United States—5,283 facilities—were cited for almost 9,000 instances of abuse from January 1999 to January 2001.

Common problems included untreated bedsores, inadequate medical care, malnutrition, dehydration, preventable accidents, and inadequate sanitation and hygiene, the report said. In 1,601 cases, the abuse violations were serious enough to cause actual harm to residents or to place them in immediate jeopardy of death or serious injury, it said.

"What we have found is shocking," said Rep. Henry Waxman, D-California, the committee's minority leader, who had instructed the staff to do the study.

Thirty percent of nursing homes across the United States cited for 9,000 instances of abuse—30 percent; that's one in three!

Imagine a restaurant with those stats. It would have to post a sign: WARNING. ONE OUT OF THREE DINERS HAS GOTTEN SICK OR DIED HERE.

Representative Waxman is from California, but his report is not about California per se. It's about all 50 states. The following is a small sample of the types of state reports included in the congressional findings, which occurred over a 48-month period. A detailed table of nursing home abuse and neglect broken down by state follows the reports.

Missouri

The report cited heat-related deaths of four elderly women in Leland Health Care Center in University City, Missouri, which occurred within a 48-hour period in April 2001. The air-conditioning was not working at the time, and these four elderly women literally baked to death on the third floor of a three-story brick building, when temperatures inside climbed to 95 degrees and higher.

Georgia

The report reveals an eyewitness account of abuse in a nursing home in Georgia. The eyewitness said, "I saw a nurse hit and yell at the lady across the hall because the nurse told the lady she didn't have all day to wait on her. The lady made some remark. The nurse hit the woman and said, 'Shut up.'"

Texas

A relative of a patient in a nursing home in Texas said, "I came in and found my mom battered and bruised. I mean, her whole face was bruised and swollen. The backs of her hands and arms were bruised as if she tried to protect herself."

Florida

Testimony from a certified nurse assistant: "The worse thing about my job is the sense of powerlessness. You see residents suffering, but you've got 15 on your hands, and you can't get to a resident. You tell the charge nurse what's going on, and she just looks at you like you're a fool and says there's nothing she can do. Yes, that hopelessness of not being able to make a difference."

California

According to government inspection records, Ensign Group nursing homes committed more violations of resident care laws than the federal and state averages. Violations committed by the Ensign Group nursing homes included: insufficient staff; failure to treat residents with dignity and respect; failure to keep residents free from neglect, physical abuse, and sexual abuse; failure to respect residents' rights; failure to develop and implement comprehensive care plans; and failure to prevent accidents.

See Table 1.1 for a state-by-state breakdown of nursing home abuse and neglect.

What this chart means: If you live in the State of Connecticut, you're in big trouble. From January 1997 to June 1998, 52 percent of nursing homes were cited for actual harm or immediate jeopardy. The period January 1999 to July 2000 is a little bit better. Only 48 percent of the homes in Connecticut were cited for actual harm or immediate jeopardy! In the period July 2000 to January 2002, Connecticut became more dangerous again; 49 percent of the nursing homes were cited for actual harm or immediate jeopardy.

Other homes that seemed to rank consistently high were in Alabama, Illinois, Iowa, Kentucky, Nebraska, Ohio, South Dakota, and Washington. Apparently, if you want to be in the safest nursing homes, you want to live in either Maine or Oklahoma.

How to read this list: If your loved one was in a nursing home in Connecticut from January 1997 to June 1998, they had a 52 percent chance of being abused. Take a look at the category called Percentage of Homes Cited for Actual Harm or Immediate Jeopardy. From July 2000 to January 2002, the numbers improved slightly. You had only a 49.4 percent chance of having your loved one abused. That represented a decrease of 4.4 percent.

Table 1.1
Nursing Home Abuse/Neglect by State

Trends in the Proportion of Nursing Homes Cited for Actual Harm or Immediate Jeopardy Deficiencies, 1999–2002

State	Number of Homes Surveyed			Percentage of Homes Cited for Actual Harm or Immediate Jeopardy			Percentage Point Difference	
	1/97–6/98	1/99–7/00	7/00–1/02	1/97–6/98	1/99–7/00	7/00–1/02	1/97–6/98 and 1/99–7/00	1/99–7/00 and 7/00–1/02
Alabama	227	225	228	51.1	42.2	18.4	-8.9	-23.8
Alaska	16	15	15	37.5	20.0	33.3	-17.5	13.3
Arizona	163	142	147	17.2	33.8	8.8	16.6	-25.0
Arkansas	285	273	267	14.7	37.7	27.3	23.0	-10.4
California	1,435	1,400	1,348	28.2	29.1	9.3	0.9	-19.9
Colorado	234	227	225	11.1	15.4	26.2	4.3	10.8
Connecticut	263	262	259	52.9	48.5	49.4	-4.0	0.9
Delaware	44	42	42	45.5	52.4	14.3	6.9	-38.1
District of Columbia	24	20	21	12.5	10.0	33.3	-2.5	23.3
Florida	730	753	742	36.3	20.8	20.1	-15.5	-0.8
Georgia	371	368	370	17.8	22.6	20.5	4.8	-2.0
Hawaii	45	47	46	24.4	25.5	15.2	1.1	-10.3
Idaho	86	83	84	55.8	54.2	13.0	-1.6	-23.3
Illinois	899	900	881	29.8	23.3	15.4	-0.5	-13.9
Indiana	602	590	573	40.5	45.3	26.2	4.8	-19.1
Iowa	525	492	494	39.2	19.3	9.9	-19.9	-9.4

State							
Kansas	445	410	400	47.0	37.1	29.0	−9.9	−8.1
Kentucky	318	312	306	28.6	28.8	25.2	0.2	−3.7
Louisiana	433	387	367	12.7	19.9	23.4	7.2	3.5
Maine	135	126	124	7.4	10.3	9.7	2.9	−0.6
Maryland	258	242	248	19.0	25.6	20.2	6.6	−5.5
Massachusetts	576	542	512	24.0	33.0	22.9	9.0	−10.2
Michigan	451	449	441	43.7	42.1	24.7	−1.6	−17.4
Minnesota	446	439	431	29.6	31.7	18.8	2.1	−12.9
Mississippi	218	202	219	24.8	33.2	19.6	8.4	−13.5
Missouri	595	584	569	21.0	22.3	10.2	1.3	−12.1
Montana	106	104	103	38.7	37.5	25.2	−1.2	−12.3
Nebraska	263	242	243	32.3	26.0	18.9	−6.3	−7.1
Nevada	49	52	51	40.8	32.7	9.8	−8.1	−22.9
New Hampshire	86	83	79	30.2	37.3	21.5	7.1	−15.8
New Jersey	377	359	366	13.0	24.5	22.4	11.5	−2.1
New Mexico	88	82	82	11.4	31.7	17.1	20.3	−14.6
New York	662	668	671	13.3	32.2	32.3	18.9	0.2
North Carolina	407	414	419	31.0	40.8	30.1	9.8	−10.7
North Dakota	88	89	88	55.7	21.3	28.4	−34.4	7.1
Ohio	1,043	1,047	1,029	31.2	29.0	23.7	−2.2	−5.3
Oklahoma	463	432	394	8.4	16.7	20.6	8.3	3.9
Oregon	171	158	152	43.9	47.5	33.6	3.6	−13.9

(Continued)

17

Table 1.1 *(Continued)*

Trends in the Proportion of Nursing Homes Cited for Actual Harm or Immediate Jeopardy Deficiencies, 1999–2002

State	Number of Homes Surveyed			Percentage of Homes Cited for Actual Harm or Immediate Jeopardy			Percentage Point Difference	
	1/97–6/98	1/99–7/00	7/00–1/02	1/97–6/98	1/99–7/00	7/00–1/02	1/97–6/98 and 1/99–7/00	1/99–7/00 and 7/00–1/02
Pennsylvania	811	788	764	29.3	32.2	11.6	2.9	−20.6
Rhode Island	102	99	99	11.8	12.1	10.1	0.3	−2.0
South Carolina	175	178	180	28.6	28.7	17.8	0.1	−10.9
South Dakota	124	112	114	40.3	24.1	30.7	−16.2	6.6
Tennessee	361	354	377	11.1	26.0	16.7	14.9	−9.3
Texas	1,381	1,336	1,275	22.2	26.9	25.5	4.7	−1.5
Utah	98	95	95	15.3	15.8	15.8	0.5	0.0
Vermont	45	46	45	20.0	15.2	17.8	−4.8	2.6
Virginia	279	287	285	24.7	19.9	11.6	−4.8	−8.3
Washington	288	279	275	63.2	54.1	38.5	−9.1	−15.6
West Virginia	130	147	143	12.3	15.6	14.0	3.3	−1.7
Wisconsin	438	428	421	17.1	14.0	7.1	−3.1	−6.9
Wyoming	38	41	40	28.9	43.9	22.5	15.0	−21.4
Nation	**17,897**	**17,452**	**17,149**	**27.7**	**29.3**	**20.5**	**1.6**	**−8.8**

By contrast, according to this chart, if you lived in Wisconsin, from January 1997 to June 1998, there was a 17 percent chance your loved one would be abused. From July 2000 to January 2002, the percentage of potential abuse was 7.1 percent, which is a decline of minus 3.1 percent or minus 6.9 percent.

In reviewing the Senate Committee Hearings on Nursing Home Abuse (which he chaired), Senator Kit Bond concluded with this observation: "Neglecting an elderly, frail individual is no different than neglecting a child. Both are defenseless and lack a strong voice. Both are vulnerable and both suffer at the hands of those who are nothing more than cowards and criminals. The findings in our report are especially timely, considering the fact that we are now entering a generation in which it is very likely that we will spend more time taking care of our elderly parents than we took taking care of our own children." The list of cited abuse in this congressional report is endless.

So, you ask yourself, "How do I make sure that this does not happen to my loved one?" We're assuming—for the time being—that your loved one is already in a nursing home, and you are looking for any signs of active or passive abuse.

Normally, active abuse is the easiest to spot and stop. If your loved one or the roommate is able to talk, they can tell you about the abuse. If they're not able to tell you, you can look for those telltale black and blue marks, and go right to the top. Report it to Adult Protective Services in your city. Report it to the state's nursing home ombudsman services—*immediately.*

If there truly is physical abuse, the nursing home staff may try to deny it or hide it. That's why you go right to the top in the case of physical abuse. To prevent it from happening again, insist that a video monitor be placed in your loved one's room.

This was one of the recommendations from U.S. Senator Kit Bond, who said, "We need new bedside technology that can easily and accurately record individual information about nursing home residents and the care they receive."

Two areas of active abuse that may not be as easy to detect involve physical restraint and chemical restraint. Some of the possible effects of physical restraint[3] are: incontinence because a restrained person cannot get to the bathroom; dehydration because a restrained person can't get anything to drink; and urinary tract infections from incontinence, lack of fluids, and not moving.

On the other hand, possible effects resulting from chemical restraints are: repetitive movements of the head and tongue, known as tardive dyskinesia; agitation—a drug intended to calm a resident has the reverse effect; and polypharmacy, which causes blood pressure to drop and leads to falls that may result in hip fractures.

When you see any of the telltale signs just mentioned, report it immediately to the supervisor.

So how do you know when your loved one has been a victim of active abuse? Here are the most common scenarios and noticeable signs.[4]

If you suspect your loved one is not being taken to the bathroom when he needs to go, ask yourself: *How often do I find him wet? Does he smell?* Also, examine his buttocks or clothes. Have dried urine or feces been there for a while? If, on the other hand, you suspect he's not getting enough fluids, ask yourself: *Does my loved one's mouth look dry? Did his tongue stick to the inside of his mouth? Did his lips appear dry, maybe even peeling slightly?* Another telltale sign of neglect is improper or insufficient grooming, which leads to poor hygiene. Ask yourself: *Does my loved one have a clean washcloth and towel? Is their toothbrush wet in the mornings and evenings, indicating use?* These are just a few of the many ways to uncover active abuse and neglect, if you suspect your loved one has fallen prey to either.

Passive abuse, on the other hand, is a bit more elusive to identify. The Government Accounting Office (GAO) has a name for these instances of abuse: "crimes of omission." Some of the worst are: failure to feed the patient; failure to hydrate the patient; failure to take the patient to the bathroom; failure to change bandages; and failure to turn the patient over, thereby alleviating bedsores.

Not surprisingly, the GAO found that the primary causes of death in nursing homes are *dehydration* and *malnutrition*. Moreover, the GAO found that nursing home inspections are infrequent and insufficient, specifically as they relate to nursing home abuse. Another challenge they found was the difficulty in reporting abuse. Residents can't report it, because they're not articulate or are cowed into silence. And many family and friends won't report, because they're afraid of retaliation. Another roadblock in uncovering nursing home abuse is that personnel will not snitch on each other.

With that said, it should now be clear that you must be very selective and scrutinizing when choosing the nursing home where your loved one will spend his final days. Furthermore, the government is not the answer to preventing nursing home abuse.

So on the clichéd principle that "An ounce of prevention is worth a pound of cure," how can you prevent you or your loved ones from getting into a nursing home situation that is abusive? Here's how.

Selecting the Right Nursing Home

Nursing homes are licensed and regulated by the state Department of Health and Social Services; therefore, all homes in the state presumably follow a uniform set of standards. However, it's up to you to find a nursing home that meets your individual needs and makes you feel safe and comfortable.

I strongly encourage that you visit the proposed nursing home as soon as possible. When you do, here's a useful checklist (Table 1.2) of what to look for. It's by no means comprehensive, so feel free to add your own categories to the list, and take it with you on your visit!

Annual Survey Report

In addition to completing a checklist, you can ask the nursing home staff to show you their annual survey report. This is an inspection report of the nursing home prepared by the state Department of Health and Social Services, Division of Health, Bureau of Quality Compliance.

The annual survey report must be posted in a prominent location in the nursing home. On the left of the report are any detailed discrepancies or explanations of code violations. On the right, the facility responds with their plan for correcting the deficiency.

Compare their annual survey report with the public nursing home reports you can find on the Internet. There are several Internet sites:

- http://www.membersofthefamily.net
- http://www.nursinghomeabuse.com
- http://www.carescout.com
- http://www.myziva.net
- http://www.medicaid.org

As a reference point, let's look at two of these: CareScout and MyZiva.

Table 1.2
Your Checklist

Location	YES	NO
Would the home be convenient for you/your loved one as a resident, or your visitors?		
Is it near a doctor's office or a cooperating hospital?		
Is it near your doctor's office?		
Staff		
How do staff members interact with residents?		
Are they readily available?		
Does staff look happy?		
Residents		
Do residents appear neat and clean?		
Can residents decorate their rooms and choose the clothes they wear?		
Are most residents out of their beds, sitting up in their bedrooms or in a day room?		
Level of Care		
Do they specialize in the care you/your loved one needs (i.e., Alzheimer's, cancer, etc.)?		
Are facilities available for any necessary therapy?		
Are other medical services provided regularly, such as dental care?		
Are there facilities to handle patients with contagious illnesses?		
What are the medical emergency/hospitalization procedures?		
Counseling		
Is counseling available to residents and their families?		
Are there specialized services for relatives with Alzheimer's disease or other disorders?		

(Continued)

Table 1.2 *(Continued)*

Safety	YES	NO
Is it easy to get around the home with assistive devices (i.e., canes, wheelchairs, etc.)?		
Are hallways wide enough for two wheelchairs to pass through easily?		
Are there grab bars on the corridor walls?		
Is the home well lit with clearly marked and unobstructed exits?		
Are emergency evacuation plans posted around the home?		
Dining		
Do the meals look appetizing?		
Do those who need help with eating get it?		
Are dining rooms comfortable and easy to get around in?		
Is there time allowed to eat?		
Can special diets be accommodated?		
Atmosphere		
Is it warm and friendly?		
Are staff members courteous, respectful, and amiable toward residents?		
Do administrators respond promptly to questions or problems?		
Comfort		
Are bedrooms comfortable and well furnished?		
Is a nurse call button by each bed?		
Is it easy to go from bed to bathroom?		
Is it easy to move around the bathroom?		
Is enough drawer and closet space provided?		

Table 1.2 *(Continued)*

Recreation	YES	NO
Are residents encouraged to take part in recreational programs?		
Can the home handle residents' hobbies?		
Are those who can go for fresh air or outside trips able to do so?		
Policies		
Does the home accept Medicaid patients?		
Are there restrictions that would prevent you from living there?		
Residents' Rights		
Does the home have a written list of residents' rights on hand?		
Is a residents' council in place?		
Are private rooms set aside for visits with family and friends?		
What about spiritual activities; can residents participate as they wish?		

Top Performing Nursing Homes in United States Picked by CareScout

A list of nursing homes selected as Top Performers in the United States was released some time ago by CareScout (http://www.care scout.com), a company that says it is "dedicated to empowering Americans with cost savings and quality of care information on nursing homes, assisted living facilities, and home health agencies nationwide."

The criteria were for quality of care performance ratings for government-certified nursing homes in the United States. Updated quarterly, CareScout assigns ratings to nursing homes by evaluating government inspection records, quality of life data, and other objective resident care information for all certified facilities.

In announcing these ratings, CareScout recognized a select number of nursing homes throughout the United States for earning a AAA current state rating in its latest ratings, the company's top performer designation, and for maintaining a four-year historical mark of consecutive AAA current state ratings. Of the 16,400 government-certified nursing home facilities in the United States, only 151 received CareScout's highest honor.

CareScout's ratings designations include AAA, AA, A, B, C, and D. To receive CareScout's top AAA state rating, nursing homes must meet exceptional quality of life and care requirements, maintain full compliance with all eldercare laws and regulations, and be free of any health deficiencies as noted by state and federal officials during the nursing home's most recent unannounced inspection survey.

Robert Bua, president and chief executive officer of CareScout, said, "We don't hear enough about the nursing homes that are doing a great job delivering care. These nursing homes demonstrably outperformed their peers on almost 200 specific quality-of-care and quality-of-life benchmarks."

New Web Site Ranks Best Nursing Homes

MyZiva.net—named after the Eastern European goddess of good health and long life—provides free information that can help you choose a nursing home. The site takes annual government surveys of all licensed facilities and presents the data in a user-friendly format. Area nursing homes can be compared side-by-side, and information boxes explain the meaning of fields such as environmental deficiencies. That category, for instance, measures a home's proficiency in providing a "safe, clean, functional and hazard-free environment."

According to the article, nursing homes may maintain a Facility Focus page on MyZiva.net for a fee of $15 per bed, linked to the main web site. This income covers the cost of maintaining the web site. One notable feature is the Performance tab, where nursing homes can provide an explanation for any deficiencies noted in the surveys. The site also contains a resource guide for consumers and a checklist of items to note when you are visiting a nursing home.

Be sure to do some digging before visiting the nursing home, so as not to waste your time. When you do decide to visit, be sure to take a walking tour of the nursing home with different personnel and during different shifts to get an idea of how the staff interacts with residents. Get to know the staff by name and talk to residents.

When you make your final decision to take your loved one to a particular nursing home, sit down with the admissions director to get them up to speed on your loved one's history, habits, preferences, and the like.

Remember, no detail is too small if it's significant to your father or mother, husband or wife. Have these things written down ahead of time to hand the director, or make sure that they write down this history of details as you disclose your loved one's personality.

How to Address Problems

If there is imminent danger to your loved one, or there is clear evidence of physical abuse, go directly to the top. We talked about this earlier. Absent danger and abuse, give the staff the benefit of the doubt with regard to other problems or minor misunderstandings. This at times will be difficult. However, no matter how outraged you are, remember that you can catch more flies with honey than you can with vinegar.

To prevent alienation, defensiveness, or outright lying on the part of the staff, first talk to the staff about the problem. If you've taken the time to get acquainted with the staff ahead of time, you'll be more capable of perceiving what really happened, thereby giving them a chance to respond appropriately. Anytime anyone's pride or professionalism is attacked, they become defensive.

If necessary, go to the head nurse and let him/her know what you want to discuss. Keep the discussion focused on solving the problem, not on placing blame. The principle always is, "Fix the problem, not the blame." Be solution oriented.

Know what you want the outcome to be, and be very specific. "I want my mother's water jug filled every hour, and I want someone to stay in there and make sure she sips every time you bring water in." "I want my mother to be escorted to the bingo room every afternoon at three." If necessary, ask a long-term care ombudsman to assist you in getting your loved one's needs met.

File a formal complaint to the state nursing home regulatory agency if needed, but before getting to that point, first meet with the owner of the nursing home and give him or her a chance to correct the problem before you file the complaint with the Better Business Bureau or with the regulator. Emotions are fragile, and sometimes businesspeople do things that are not in their best interests or the best interests of their customers simply out of pride.

Nevertheless, your focus is this: Do you want to succeed or do you want to have your own way? If you want to have your own way, you can scream and demand or file complaints. If you want to succeed (i.e., get a safe, healthy environment for your loved one), then see if you can get voluntary cooperation from the owner. Tell him or her, "I was going to file a complaint with the Better Business Bureau, the state Department of Health, and the National Care Alliance, but before I did that, I wanted to give you the benefit of the doubt, because I assume that you are unaware of some of these problems."

When reporting a problem, let the staff member or the nurse give their side of the story. Even if you suspect they're lying or being defensive, let them talk. Let them get it all out. If that doesn't bring about a solution, then go directly to the owner of the home. If that doesn't take care of it, then you go directly to the state and the local Adult Protective Services, as well as to the media.

These steps may seem trivial and cumbersome. But in the end, they can save you and your loved one unnecessary heartache, like what happened to April, my client and friend.

April had been Charlotte's best friend from the age of 10. Although April had moved to the suburbs 40 years ago, they still talked a couple of times a week by phone. Even though April didn't live nearby, she often knew the hometown gossip, days before her friend did.

April had a series of strokes, each leaving her more paralyzed. Her husband Cedric transformed their home into an accessible mini-hospital. Although April was depressed by her condition, she would be all made up, her hair just so, ready to play the hostess role for Charlotte's visits.

Cedric's third hernia operation led to a six-week convalescence. The home health aide quit, unable to handle total care for April without Cedric's help. Without other options, Cedric arranged for April to be admitted to a nearby nursing home with a good reputation. He took her there the next day.

Charlotte visited the nursing home the following weekend, braced for the worst. When she'd spoken to April before she moved, April made it clear she didn't want to go. When Charlotte called her at the nursing home, the staff said she couldn't come to the phone.

Walking in the front door, Charlotte found a crowd of people in wheelchairs, some staring blankly into space, others slumped in their chairs. All seemed to be waiting, but for what it wasn't clear. Not finding April, Charlotte looked for a staff person to direct her to April's room. A woman touched her arm as Charlotte walked past. Charlotte turned and looked. "April?" she asked in disbelief. April's hair was combed but had none of its usual flair. Without makeup, her face was ghostly pale. Awkwardly positioned, April was unable to adjust herself to look straight at Charlotte so she tilted her head—and burst into tears.

Charlotte hugged and soothed her friend, and asked one of the aides for a place where they could talk privately. They were directed to a room down the hall. April was too worried about her husband Cedric. "I haven't heard from him all day. Where is he? I know something's wrong. I just know he's lying on the floor."

"I'll call him for you," Charlotte said. "And I'll find out what's going on. But first, let's take you some place where we can talk." After Charlotte found the pay phone and learned that Cedric was okay, she reported to April.

The two friends talked for a while. About 4:30, April had to go to the bathroom. It took half an hour to get assistance because the staff members were rushing around with the medications and the trays for the evening meal. Eventually, someone helped her and then they were able to go to the dining room for dinner.

April said she didn't have an appetite and that she hadn't eaten since she'd arrived. After reminding April to eat to keep up her strength, Charlotte realized that the real problem wasn't one of the will, but of the way. This night's main course was pasta twirls, a challenge for the most able-bodied eaters, but a frustrating embarrassment for a naturally right-handed person now forced to eat with her left hand. As food landed in her lap, April apologized for her mess. The one aide in the room appeared overwhelmed assisting people to and from their tables. Most of those in the dining room had no one to help them eat.

Charlotte coaxed and fed her friend, helping her to get most of the meal down. April wouldn't drink the whole milk offered; she was used to low-fat milk. April lamented that she was supposed to be on a low-cholesterol, low-fat diet, but the home's physician had issued orders for a regular diet.

April's tablemate was cheerful and warm, and with Charlotte's prompting, they struck up a conversation. As they left the dining room, Charlotte sought some reassurance that the woman would eat with April again, and then took her friend back to her room. "Please, get me out of here," April pleaded, amid tears, hugs, apologies, and thanks.

On subsequent visits, Charlotte found that the situation hadn't improved for April. She withdrew, grew weaker, and lost her spirit.

In lots of little ways, this good nursing home contributed to April's deterioration. But it didn't have to be that way.

If Charlotte had known how to advocate for her friend, she could have helped bring concerns to the attention of the staff. With proper assessment and care planning, the situation could have improved. Staff would have known enough about April to individualize her care and her routines. If this nursing home had connected with April, they would have known.

April's connection to the outside world, via the telephone, was critical to her morale. Therefore, extra efforts would have been made to get phone calls through to her and assist her in making calls. Staff would have talked with April about the possibility of having a phone by her bedside, as she'd had in her own home.

They would also know that April's spirits were always directly linked to her appearance. Staff would have helped her maintain her hairstyle and makeup, as a basic part of her grooming. They would know these were essential to her well-being.

It would have been clear to staff that April required assistance to eat and a diet suited to her individual nutritional needs and restrictions. She needed meals to accommodate her limited left-handed abilities, occupational therapy to increase the agility of her left hand, and silverware suitable for her unsteady grip.

Lastly, had the staff taken the time to get acquainted, they would have known that April thrived on social contact and needed help making friends. If she could have been actively engaged in meaningful relationships, she would have managed to feel less lonely and isolated, more comfortable, and at home.

Nursing homes have become very creative and aggressive in hiding their mistakes and preventing exposure. One nursing home in Wisconsin went so far as to put a restraining order on Norm and Shirley Matzek of Hudson, Wisconsin, forbidding them from coming to see their parents anymore! The home got tired of the Matzeks pointing out the negligence of the nursing home, so they had a lawyer tell the Matzeks they couldn't visit their own parents anymore. Their full story was written by Barbara Basler and published in the November 2004 issue of the *AARP Bulletin*, under the title "Battle of the Banned."

When the *AARP Bulletin* contacted the Christian Community Home, Administrator Dan Goodier replied in writing that the home had obtained the restraining order "as a last resort after exhausting our internal efforts to address the Matzeks' disruptive and intimidating behavior."

"Nursing homes have themselves used intimidation as a tool for years," says Toby Edelman, an attorney with the Washington office of the Center for Medicare Advocacy, "but today, families are better informed and more aggressive about demanding good care, so we're hearing more about it."

Another sensitive issue among nursing homes is staffing. Government studies indicate that 90 percent of the nation's nursing homes are understaffed. This may explain why more and more homes (like the Matzeks' case) are increasingly defensive about complaints.

Since the issue of the restraining order in December 2002, the Matzeks have spent more than $30,000 in legal fees trying to get the temporary restraining order lifted. AARP filed a friend of the court brief in their case, arguing against the order and for the Matzeks' rights.

In the meantime, Norm's mother died one night after 8:30 P.M.—the visiting deadline imposed by the restraining order. Although the home offered to let the Matzeks stay, "the atmosphere was so intimidating, we left," Norm says. "She died later that night, without us. That was so hard, so sad, just so wrong."

The Nursing Home Dilemma

In a new crackdown on substandard care, federal officials have imposed fines on hundreds of nursing homes across the country, and courts have upheld penalties of more than $1,000 a day for each violation.

Some nursing homes have been accused of filing false claims for federal medical insurance when they harmed patients by not meeting federal standards.

The United States Court of Appeals for the 10th Circuit, in Denver, recently upheld a penalty of $1,300 a day against a Utah nursing home that had allowed patients to develop pressure sores, or bedsores. The court said the fine was "appropriate and reasonable" because the home, the South Valley Health Care Center in West Jordan, Utah, had caused harm to patients by flouting federal standards.

In another case, Beechknoll Convalescent Center in Cincinnati was fined $153,000. The government said the home had failed to respect patients' privacy rights and to care properly for patients suffering from pressure sores, infections, and incontinence. The home is contesting the fine.

Doctors and nurses consider bedsores potentially serious problems because, if neglected, they can damage surrounding tissue, extend deep into the muscle and bone, and cause long hospital stays.

In recent lawsuits against three nursing homes in Philadelphia, the government said the homes had filed "false, fictitious or fraudulent claims" because they did not provide the nursing, nutrition, and other services they had promised.

David R. Hoffman, an assistant United States attorney in Philadelphia, said, "The common thread in these cases is that nursing home residents received grossly inadequate care. They were profoundly malnourished, lost significant amounts of weight and developed pressure ulcers that did not heal and were not treated."

As I mentioned, there are several ways to investigate a prospective nursing home. One of the most popular is to check them out online. The federal government has posted evaluations of most nursing homes at http://www.medicare.gov, which include inspection reports.

Here is an overview of what a nursing home inspector's snapshot report should include:

- *General Information.* Each facility's address, county, phone number, and last inspection date as well as Number of Beds, Number of Residents, Number of Occupied Beds, Percentage of Beds Occupied, Accepts Medicare/Medicaid or Both, Resident and/or Family Councils Present, Type of Ownership, if Located within a Hospital, if Part of a Multi-home Chain.

- *Resident Condition.* This graph shows the average percentage of residents with at least one of several specific conditions: Physical Restraints, With Infections, With Pain, With Pain (Short Stay).
- *Nursing Home Staffing.* This area shows the average number of staff hours worked each day by RNs, LPNs/LVNs, and CNAs divided by the number of residents. This is a good measure of the trained medical staff available, on average, for comparison purposes.
- *Inspection Deficiencies.* Total Deficiency Ratings for the facility are compared graphically to county, state, and national averages. A historical summary for these scores is also provided by inspection date.

Each deficiency reported is assigned a Scope and Level of Harm rating by the inspector. Ratings are then assigned a progressive Deficiency Rating (see Table 1.3).

In this manner, the scores, or point values, assigned to each deficiency may be compared with others or combined to directly

Table 1.3
Deficiency Rating

Severity	Scope	Level of Harm
0	Not available	Not available
2	1-Isolated	1-Potential for minimal harm
3	2-Pattern	1-Potential for minimal harm
3	1-Isolated	2-Minimal harm or potential for actual harm
4	3-Widespread	1-Potential for minimal harm
4	2-Pattern	2-Minimal harm or potential for actual harm
5	3-Widespread	2-Minimal harm or potential for actual harm
5	2-Pattern	3-Actual harm
5	1-Isolated	4-Immediate jeopardy to resident health or safety
6	3-Widespread	3-Actual harm
6	2-Pattern	4-Immediate jeopardy to resident health or safety
7	3-Widespread	4-Immediate jeopardy to resident health or safety

compare deficiencies by: Category, Total Facility Score, scores by County—State—USA, and Total Score History by Inspection Date.

Here is a description of what the Nursing Home Inspector Detail Report should look like.

The Nursing Home Inspector Detail Report displays all the elements found in the SnapShot Report plus more extensive statistics and descriptions including accounts of each deficiency and a history of deficiencies reported.

The Detail Report is broken down into six primary areas:

1. About the Home.
2. About the Residents.
3. About the Staff.
4. About State Inspection Deficiencies.
5. Inspection Deficiency Details.
6. Complaint Investigation Deficiencies.

About the Home

As in the SnapShot Report, each facility's address and statistics about Beds, Occupancy, Medicare/Medicaid Acceptance, Councils, and Ownership are displayed.

About the Residents

This graph shows the average percentage of residents with at least one of several specific conditions: Physical Restraints, With Infections, With Pain, With Pain (Short Stay).

About the Staff

This area shows the average number of staff hours worked each day by RNs, LPNs/LVNs and CNAs divided by the number of residents. This is a good measure of the trained medical staff available, on average, for comparison purposes.

About State Inspection Deficiencies

Each deficiency reported is assigned a Scope and Level of Harm rating by the inspectors. These ratings are then assigned a progressive Deficiency Rating. In this manner the deficiency scores, or point values, assigned may be compared to each other or combined to directly compare deficiencies by: Category, Total Facility Score, Average Scores by Region, and Total Score History. Ratings are compared graphically to County, State, and USA averages. A graphic history of the Total Deficiency Ratings for this facility are also displayed for trend indication.

A chart is displayed with total deficiency scores broken down by Category and Inspection Date. A pop-up detail is available showing all deficiencies reported for each Category for the past three inspections and for each inspection individually.

Inspection Deficiency Details

A detailed account is provided for each deficiency cited during the past three inspections. Each detail provides the Date Cited, Category, Scope, Level of Harm, Deficiency Rating, and a text description of the deficiency.

Complaint Investigation Deficiencies

Complaints that are substantiated by the state survey agency are investigated by inspectors. All complaints resulting in a deficiency are reported and included in this section by date.

Visit your proposed nursing home (or nursing homes) at random.

- *How does the nursing home relate to residents?* Is the worker friendly to other residents? If not, you may want to ask the administrator about this particular person. If the worker mistreats, in any way, another resident that worker may do it to your loved one.
- *How does the nursing home greet you?* Is the staff friendly and helpful to you?
- *How does the nursing home respond to your questions?* You may have questions for the facility when you visit or call your loved one. If the worker does not know the answer, is he or she willing to ask someone who can help you? How do they respond to your question? For instance, if you suspect that a worker is not properly treating your loved one, do they defend that worker or do they immediately get someone whom you can talk to?

Nursing homes should tell you anything that you would like to know. There should be no excuses. If you have guardianship, it is your right to be told *anything* that you want to know about the care of your loved one.

Preparing Your Loved One for a Nursing Home

When you've tentatively selected a nursing home, visit for a day appointment with your loved one. If your loved one is able, have him or her eat lunch, play bingo, take a tour with other residents. Frequently, your loved one will find common interests with other residents. This facilitates acceptance of the new home.

In spite of your best preparations, your loved one may still have difficulty adjusting. He or she may: call you throughout the day; cry; not eat; be depressed; and/or show challenging behaviors (i.e., acting out).

At the same time, while your loved one goes through the process of adapting to a nursing home, he or she may feel:

- Upset
- Lonely
- Depressed
- Scared
- Worried

Do not give in and take him or her back home (unless it's a clear case of abuse). *Do* visit and call frequently, at different times throughout the day.

When your loved one is in a nursing home, these are the items to watch for:

- *How does your loved one feel?* I listed many feelings that your loved one may have while in a nursing home: upset, lonely, depressed, scared, worried. While visiting your loved one, encourage him or her to talk about feelings. He or she may not be getting enough attention or may not be participating in activities. There is usually an underlying reason why your loved one feels a certain way.
- *How does your loved one look?* Self-image is extremely important, especially if you've known your loved one to be fashion sensitive. Feeling good about appearance makes one feel good all over. The home should honor this by allowing the loved one to wear his or her own clothes and to have his or her hair and nails done. If you notice that this is not happening, report it immediately.

- *Has your loved one changed dramatically within a short period of time?* It is only natural that little changes will occur, but they shouldn't be dramatic.
- *Is your loved one receiving the appropriate exercises and recreational activities?* Nursing homes should promote health and well-being by providing daily exercises and recreational activities for your loved one. The home should be experienced in alternating its exercises and activities to fit your loved one's needs.

  If your loved one is in a wheelchair, he/she can still join in. If your loved one is bedridden, the home can have someone visit your loved one and do in-bed exercises.

In short, the nursing home should respect all the patients' rights, listed earlier in this chapter.

Who can help to make sure abuses are eliminated and rights are respected?

- Caregivers whose loved one is currently in a nursing home.
- Caregivers whose loved one used to be in a nursing home.
- Caregivers who decided not to place their loved one in a nursing home.
- Caregivers who saw/heard things in a nursing home while visiting their loved one.
- Other family or friends who have visited someone in a nursing home.
- Persons who are currently working or volunteering in a nursing home.
- Persons who have worked or volunteered in a nursing home.
- Any visitor to a nursing home or assisted living center.

How can you help? You can help by expressing your joys, concerns, and/or fears of nursing homes. You may have had excellent experiences with nursing home facilities, or you may have had not so good experiences. My hope is to educate caregivers on what may or may not occur in nursing homes by providing them with firsthand experiences as well as helpful tips when they are seeking out a proper facility. Feel free to share your experiences.

Write me at P.O. Box 814514, Dallas, TX 75381.

CHAPTER SUMMARY

We've read in this chapter that nursing home experiences are unpleasant at best and lethal at worst. We've also read that nursing home abuse is systemic and cannot be prevented or corrected merely by government regulations. We've also read that in many cases, nursing home abuse is silent, meaning that by the time you find out a loved one has been abused, it's too late. Death or permanent injury may have occurred.

So what do you do with this information?

ACTION STEPS

❑ Admit that someday you or a loved one will reach a point where performing the Activities of Daily Living independently will not be possible. At some point, you'll need professional help. Don't look for the government to provide that professional help.

❑ Be sure to use the strategies outlined earlier (i.e., checklist) to check on the nursing home you choose for your loved one ahead of time.

❑ If your loved one is in a nursing home now, be proactive and use the suggestions we discussed in this chapter to monitor the nursing home.

❑ Do take the time to visit your loved one(s) in the nursing home to ensure that they are receiving the proper care.
❑ If you're a health care provider, always remember the Golden Rule. One of these days, you'll be the one on the receiving end, unable to do for yourself.

CONCLUSION

In light of the negligence in nursing homes and the fear of nursing homes that we documented in this chapter, why do millions still surrender to nursing homes year after year after year?

The answer is denials and delays.

CHAPTER 2

The Problem:
Denials and Delays

The number one mistake is failing to consider long-term care needs.
—"Cracks in Nest Egg," the
Wall Street Journal, October 22, 2001

Within the next few years, one out of three of us will be caring for an elderly citizen.
—Dr. Claude Amarnick,
psychologist, gerontologist

I DIDN'T KNOW ARLENE WAS HAULING IN HER SON JEFF. HANDS AS BIG as hams, fingers thick as thumbs, and stomach bulging like a beer keg, Jeff yells at me, "Why didn't you do something! Why didn't you help Momma and Daddy!"

Jeff locks his chubby fingers together, slams them on my round, cherry-wood table, and leans over to stare at me with cobalt eyes.

I look at Arlene. She's settled back in her chair, shoulders drooped, head down. She has one arm collapsed on the table, the other cradled in the space between her legs, resting on her Wal-Mart flower-print dress.

"It's time, Doc," she says softly, "to get Vic that long-term protection insurance. The doctor said yesterday that he's got it . . .
the early stages of Alzheimer's. I called yesterday and one of
your people said it's probably too late; but she said I'd have to
talk to you."

"Be right back."

I walk into my secretary's office and pull out database notes. I
return to Arlene and smoldering Jeff.

"Arlene, two years ago—when you and Vic were in here for an
appointment—I showed you long-term care—$22\frac{1}{2}$ months ago,
actually. I showed you both the same thing."

"Oh, I know, I know." She stares at her shoelaces as if she'll
find the answer in a tangle of knots. "But we didn't need it then."

When Jeff hears this bizarre reasoning from Momma, he
melts.

I had heard that same bizarre reason from Dedra.

"Doc, I'm healthy—never had a problem. There's no sense in
putting out dollars for something I don't need."

The loony logic of Arlene and Dedra's thinking is no worse
than saying, "When my house burns down, I'll take out home-
owner's insurance," or "When my car's smashed, I'll take out car
insurance."

I feel scared when I hear comments like Arlene's and Dedra's
because they invite financial disaster, family torment, and emotional collapse. These folks are in denial and in danger.

On the other hand, I feel relieved when I get a call from someone like Laura Wilson. "Doc, Brian had a series of ministrokes
yesterday. I know I can't take care of him, and the hospital said
they won't keep him more than a couple of days. They say he's
stable and he'll be okay with maintenance care for now. Joni and
Sandra live too far away to help, and Tricia—well, you know, Tricia lives in Arlington. She'll come over and help, but I can't—I

won't—ask her. She's got her own kids to take care of. How soon can I get that long-term care help started—that insurance we took out with you three years ago?"

"Immediately, Laura, immediately."

Laura triumphed because she had taken preventative action.

I love to tell clients, "Don't worry. You're protected because years ago, you were smart and you called us. You did the right thing and got your long-term care (LTC) insurance."

I hate to tell clients, "Sorry. It's too late."

For Arlene, it is too late. For Dedra, it may be too late—if she doesn't act now. Dedra's problem? She doesn't know that the cost of long-term care is the greatest threat to middle-class Americans, and she doesn't know there's a solution to this problem. She can be cared for at home during her final days. Long-term care insurance does not commit her or obligate her to a long-term care facility. Long-term care insurance will pay for her home health care.

Done right, long-term care insurance is "anti-nursing home insurance."

Long-Term Care (LTC): Why, When, Where, Who— and One Way to Stay Out of a Nursing Home

You need long-term care (LTC—same initials as Loving Tender Care) for a sustained illness or injury. This could be a broken hip, stroke, dementia, heart attack, Alzheimer's, post-surgery recovery, cancer, multiple sclerosis, or any number of other conditions.

The need for LTC can occur at any age, but it increases, as we get older. At age 65+, you're flipping a coin. At 65+, you have a 50/50 chance of needing LTC. As you read previously, President George W. Bush said that the numbers of elderly needing long-term care will more than double in the next 50 years. That's your parents, and *that's you.*

That's why I tell clients to get their LTC insurance early; it can pay for *home health care, assisted living,* or a *nursing home.* I also tell them to get their protective documents together early. These two simple strategies *do* provide peace of mind.

History

Here's how the LTC crisis arose. Years ago, insurance companies published for doctors and hospitals its list of Diagnostic Related Groups (DRGs). This list *tells* doctors and hospitals: "We will pay for only so many days and so much treatment for a given illness or injury. After that, kick the patient out, because we won't pay!"

Fact: Insurance companies pay until you get *stable*, not well. "Stable" means your vital signs are okay. That's it. You may be hobbling or bedridden. You may need help bathing, eating, walking, changing bandages, or monitoring medications. This is custodial care. It's expensive, and *you* pay for it.

Your hospital policy will not pay for it. Medicare will not pay for it. You may need the services of: an extended care center, assisted living center, or a nursing home, or you just may need care in your own home environment, which would require daily visits from care providers. Regardless of the need, you pay for it.

Where will you get the money? Let's see how most people plan. They don't. They don't think about it until it's too late. That's why I wrote this book: It's my two-by-four to smack you right on the bridge of your nose to get your attention.

The truth of the matter is that only two kinds of people don't need LTC insurance: the very rich and the very poor.

The Very Rich

Bill Gates does not need LTC plans. He could *own* every custo-dial care company, assisted living, or nursing home center in the country. He could pay for home health care until the fourth millennium.

Wait, wait, wait. I just remembered. I know a guy whose net worth is $8 million. He's an oil boss in Dallas with plenty of dough. He *still* bought LTC insurance. He knows that home health care or nursing home care costs $72,000 to $100,000 a year for him and his wife. An extended illness or injury, with 10–15 years of rehabilitation or therapy, can take $1.5 to $2 million from his estate.

"Reckon," he says, "I'll spend the $100 or $200 now for monthly insurance instead of $1 to $2 million later."

The Very Poor

If you live in a box under I-95 or I-240, or you alternate your nights among the Presbyterian Night Shelter, the Catholic Chari-ties, and the Salvation Army, you don't need LTC insurance. And if you have less than $2,000 in assets, you qualify for the govern-ment's welfare program—Medicaid. You'll get the institutional care originally designed for those who are homeless or on wel-fare. (I discuss the controversy of Medicaid planning and welfare in Chapter 5.)

For all the rest of us, between *very rich* and *very poor*, let's look at some of the common choices and clichés, which I hear too often.

Some people make the following assumption: "My health in-surance will take care of me." We've been through this one. In-surance companies boot you out of your hospital bed. As soon as you're stable, you're on your own, baby. Health insurance does not pay for long-term care.

Another cliché is, "Medicare will take care of me." Medicare is a government-sponsored, hospital insurance plan. It does *not* pay for long-term care—with one exception. It does pay (1) for the first 20 days in a nursing home/assisted living and (2) only if it is skilled care (no custodial care, no general health maintenance). After 20 days, you're on your own.

Along the same lines, some people make the assumption that "Medicaid will take care of me." Medicaid is *not* Medicare. *Medicare* (and Social Security) are "entitlement programs" you see on your payroll stubs that you paid taxes for during your working life. You paid these taxes so you could receive benefits at retirement—benefits you and your family were entitled to. *Medicaid*, by contrast, is a welfare program funded through federal and state taxes, *not through payroll taxes*. There is no entitlement.

Another flawed cliché is, "My savings will take care of me." The national average is $40,000 to $50,000 a year for a decent nursing home, assisted living, or home health care. Let's use $45,000 as our average number. That's $90,000 for a husband and wife each year. At that rate, you'll go through your $400,000 portfolio of stocks, bonds, CDs, real estate, and mutual funds mighty fast. Then, you'll go on Medicaid (welfare).

Maggie's Story[1]

Just a year after her husband died in 1999, Mary Cruice suffered a cerebral hemorrhage that left her needing round-the-clock nursing home care. Now 89, she's in a chronic, vegetative state. Her daughter, Maggie D'Alesio of Drexel Hill, Pennsylvania, drew down her mother's $100,000 in savings (mostly from the sale of the family home) to pay the bills. It was gone in less than three years.

D'Alesio is an only child—there are no siblings to share the burden. And she and her husband Rudy have five children of their own—three still at home. She's a nurse. Rudy is a police officer. There was little choice but to start filling out paperwork for Medicaid, the government program that provides health care for the poor. Now, Cruice's Social Security and her late husband's pension pay about half of the $5,000-per-month cost; Medicaid covers the rest, with a tiny allowance of $10 per month for personal expenses.

To get that help, D'Alesio spent three months navigating a bureaucratic maze to prove to the government that her mother was essentially impoverished. To qualify for Medicaid, nursing home residents usually must show no more than $2,000 in assets. Aside from gathering checking- and savings-account statements, and showing that investment accounts had been depleted, D'Alesio had to track down a 70-year-old life insurance policy to prove that it had been cashed in. "It was a nightmare of paperwork," she recalls. "Whatever my mother had in 2000, I had to show where it went in 2001, and where it was every year thereafter—including the year she went on welfare [in order to qualify for Medicaid]."

Maggie's story displays the danger of assuming that a parent's savings will take care of long-term care. It is also wrong to assume that your children's savings will take care of you.

Granted, our adult kids are well-intentioned. "Momma's never going in a nursing home while I'm alive." But unless you're wealthy and have $40,000 a year for home health care for Momma, you *will* be the one caring for her. You don't have the energy, time, skill, or money to do it.

You're the adult kid and the *caregiver*, well-intentioned and devoted—good for you! America needs a million more (*10 million* more) devoted adult kids who love and respect their parents and want to care for them. But the care boomerangs.

Attorney Harley Gordon said it right: "The family that tries to care at home for chronically-ill family members becomes a chronically-ill family."

Reality I

Statistics show that in most cases, the caregiver (that's you) *dies before the care receiver* (that's Momma). The caregiver dies from sheer exhaustion. You wear out—emotionally, physically, and financially. So, Momma ends up going into a nursing home *anyway*, with a stranger caring for her—the very thing you wanted to avoid.

Reality II

I did family counseling for many years and witnessed this: Daughter starts taking care of Momma. Daughter gets worn out. She's emotionally, physically, and financially spent.

Statistics say that 90 percent of the time, the caretaker is a woman. It's the daughter, daughter-in-law, mother, niece, and so on. Whether she's rich, poor, single, strong, sick, widowed, or divorced (or has a house full of kids), she takes on the role of caretaker.

Daughter leaves work early to care for Momma. She rises at 2:00 A.M. every day to care for Momma. As a result, her husband suffers, her kids drift, and her career bombs. (Labor statistic: 12 percent of women caregivers have to quit their jobs at the height of their careers in order to take care of their loved one.)

Daughter sinks into fatigue—she can't help it. Fatigue begins the cycle: Daughter begins to resent Momma. Daughter feels guilty for her resentment. To compensate for her feelings of resentment, daughter works *harder* to care for Momma. Daughter is now overcome with fatigue (more work = more stress = more fatigue). Hate wells up within her—unplanned, unwanted, and un-

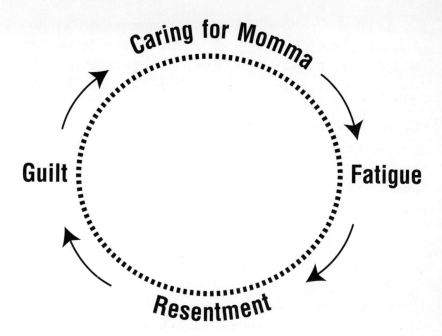

Figure 2.1　A Vicious Circle

welcome, which leads to more guilt . . . more determination to work harder—a "vicious circle." See Figure 2.1.

As demands for care increase, the wheel goes faster and faster, and deeper and deeper into a muddy rut of despair. The wheel stops only when Daughter dies, Momma dies, or Daughter hires good help for home care, or nursing home care. But how does she do that with limited assets?

The truth of the matter is you shouldn't assume your kids will take care of you. There are several reasons for that. First, they may not have the *energy*. These children, they're not spring chickens themselves anymore. Big Bicep Son is now Belly-Bustin' Son, age 52. Dynamic Daughter is now Depressed Daughter, age 48. And let's not forget that son and daughter are taking care of their own kids.

Second, they may not have the *assets*. They're paying for their own health care, their children's college expenses, and a retirement fund. Where are they going to get the money to take care of you? *Most importantly, they may not have the time.* They're working two jobs and raising two kids. Where's the time for you? And lastly, they may not live in the ideal *location.* You live in Florida. They live in California—do the math.

Let me share with you the story of my client Irene, whose mother Rachel made that very assumption, "My children will take care of me." Better yet, let *Irene* tell it—the story of a family whose parents assumed, "Hey, we always took care of our kids; they'll take care of us. . . ."

Dr. Gallagher,

Over the past three-and-a-half years, my husband and I have watched in horror as my lively mother Rachel descended into that bizarre fog called Alzheimer's. To help pay for her care, Dr. Gallagher, I contribute $1,555 a month. That's about 40 percent of my salary as a teacher. My husband and I have totally altered our lifestyle. We want to keep her in her home as long as we can, so we've hired home health care aides. Mama's Social Security and a little pension, plus our $1,555 make up the $4,860 that it costs to keep home health care aides there.

The school system better give us a raise this year, because I'm going to have to pass on that raise to the aides. It's funny. My family did everything right. My parents did everything right. They raised a family, paid off the mortgage, took us to church, raised us right, kept a clean credit record, but they forgot to plan for long-term care. We'll have to sell her home soon and then find an Alzheimer's place for her, and all the money from her home—money which I know she wanted to go to the grandkids is going to go for nursing home care. How I wish we'd talked about the whole financial situation, Dr. Gallagher!

If my mother ever knew I was spending all this money—
our money and her money—she'd scream. That's something she never wanted.

Another misconception people have is that their spouse will
take care of them, and vice versa. In fact, were you to ask your
spouse right now, they would say yes without a second thought.
They say so because they love you. They believe that under *their*
care, you will get the best care. That's noble. But what if your assumption (and theirs) is wrong?

Try this: Tell your spouse to lie in bed, as dead weight: a sack
of cement. Lift them out of bed. Guide them to the bathroom.
Lower them into the tub, lift them out, and dry them. Sit them
on the potty, lift them up, and wipe them.

Can't do it?

If you can't do it now, how will you do it when you're both
older and weaker? The care he will need—at some point—is *professional care.*

Oh, you *insist* that care take place at home? Good! Get LTC insurance, which covers home health care, and assisted living care,
and nursing home care.

In *Kiplinger's Personal Finance* magazine, Mary Beth Franklin
summed it:

"Given a choice, most people prefer to receive care in their
home . . . another option seldom covered by Medicaid. Purchasing
long-term care insurance, with the right benefits, means *you* decide
where you will receive care while protecting your life's savings."

This is how you stay out of a nursing home! You have the
money, provided by your LTC policy, which pays for your home
health care. With home health care, you keep your loved one at
home, in a safe, cozy, healthy, and familiar environment—with
professional care. This is what your loved one needs. This is what
you need. The time is coming when you or your loved one will

need help with the activities of daily living: eating, bathing, dressing, toileting, walking, and so on, and the best place to take care of these needs is at home.

Remember Henry Wadsworth Longfellow's statement: *"Stay . . . stay at home and rest. Homekeeping hearts are the happiest."*

The most flawed cliché I hear all too often is, "I'm too young to buy long-term care insurance." Ask Sam Parsons if he was too young. After he left his position at a packing company, Sam—who'd listened to my radio show—asked me to assist him in an IRA rollover of $150,000. He was 46, single, and appeared healthy. When we did the rollover, I hesitated to tell him about long-term care. *He's only 46,* I thought; but then I remembered what I told audiences and what I state in this book: My goal is to help others at all ages be accountable for their money and health decisions. My life's focus, passion, and crusade for 20 years has been to help others retire safe, early, and happy.

The mission statement we say aloud each morning at Gallagher Financial Group, Inc. (GFG, Inc.) is this: "Our mission is to be a vehicle of God's peace and comfort to as many people as possible, helping first with their financial peace of mind and also with their family, spiritual, and emotional well-being."

And this profoundly includes long-term care education.

So I gave Sam the information about long-term care, including a questionnaire, quotes, and an application. Surprisingly, he decided to take it out. At his age, it was real cheap, and it just seemed to be an extra protective measure. One year later, Sam— still feeling healthy—went for a routine physical and discovered he had an inoperable, incurable, rare form of cancer, the treatment of which would require a relatively short stay in a hospital and a l-o-n-g stay in a nursing home and rehabilitative center. Ultimately, he would need custodial care.

Thank God for Sam's common sense. Because he took out

the long-term care insurance, he'll be cared for financially the rest of his life.

Remember, health insurance does not pay for a 46-year-old who will need custodial or rehabilitative care. Health insurance does not pay for the 28-year-old who's in a coma after an automobile accident. Health insurance does not pay for a 37-year-old child, brain-dead because of a drowning accident. Health insurance does not pay for a Superman who falls off a horse, paralyzing him from the neck down.

Terminal conditions can attack us *at any age*. The fact is, more than 40 percent of Americans receiving long-term care are under 65 years old. Younger people typically need long-term care for automobile accidents, sporting accidents, brain tumors, muscular dystrophy, Parkinson's disease, Lou Gehrig's disease, and many others.

Another common misconception is, "I'm healthy, so I don't need long-term care insurance." It is precisely because you are healthy that you need long-term care insurance *now*. Think about it. No one is going to insure you *after* you get a condition that requires home health care, assisted living, or a nursing home. That was the problem with Arlene and Vic, whom I discussed on the first page of this chapter.

The bottom line is that clichés give no comfort when crisis strikes. The *Wall Street Journal* ran an excellent article, widely circulated in health, financial, legal, and popular journals: "The Ten Cracks in Your Nest Egg." Do you know what they said is the number-one crack? You guessed it: failure to provide for long-term care needs.

Recap of Important Points and Urgent Concerns

Long-term care (LTC) is the day-in, day-out assistance one needs when one has a serious illness or disability that lasts for an extended period, and is not able to take care of himself or herself. LTC includes a wide range of services delivered in adult day care centers, assisted living facilities, continuing care communities, nursing homes, or *your own home.*

The level of care is usually custodial. Custodial care may be needed for a number of reasons: injury, illness, a chronic condition, or the frailty of aging. Custodial care assists individuals with activities of daily living (ADLs), such as bathing, dressing, feeding, mobility, toileting, taking medications, or incontinence. No health insurance pays for custodial care.

Long-term care insurance (LTCI) is *anti-nursing home insurance* because with LTCI in place, you may never have to go to a nursing home. You do not want the potential isolation, abandonment, neglect, and abuse associated with a nursing home. LTCI is probably the best way to pay for that inevitable custodial care, which will allow you to stay at home.

The bottom line is: A properly structured LTCI policy is critical to sound financial planning. Once you decide to use LTCI as a means to help protect your assets, preserve choices, and maintain your family's lifestyle, it is important to obtain coverage at the earliest possible time. The cost of waiting is high, as LTCI premiums are based upon your age at the time you apply for coverage—as well as your medical history.

Paying for Long-Term Care

The cost of long-term care insurance for husband and wife can run anywhere from $100 to $300 a month. Let's use an average of $150. You may be wondering, Where do you get the $150? Well, you like to eat out, right? Depending on where you live, you're not going to get to eat out for any less than $10 each, so that's $20. If you eliminate eating out just once a day for seven days, that's $140. Based on your age, elimination period, and benefits elected, $140 could cover a premium cost for you and your spouse.

Additionally, financially comfortable middle-agers often help parents with a few bucks here and there to supplement retirement. That's good and commendable. Keep it up! And while you're at it, buy an LTCI policy for your parents.

Think about it. If the need arises for home health care, assisted living, or nursing home care, a policy paid for earlier by you and your brothers and sisters could eliminate the dilemma of deciding between low quality care for your parents and back to zero for you. Long-term care insurance is *protection for you and your parents.*

For some middle-agers, the $150 a month they pay for their parents' LTCI is "portfolio insurance" for *them*. In other words, if the parents have their LTC needs paid for, then caring for their parents will neither exhaust their savings nor deplete their portfolio, which means there'll be more money inherited by the kids, the grandkids, and so on.

Business owners can pay for long-term care insurance for their employees and for the employees' parents. This may be a deductible expense for the business and is definitely a savvy business decision for the employer. It has been shown that an employee who takes care of an elderly parent is 30 percent less efficient than an employee who does not have to for two reasons. First, a person who has to take care of parents is out a lot. When they *are* there, their work is constantly interrupted by phone calls, errands, or instant rescue missions home or to the nursing home. Second, an employee caring for an elderly parent is not alert. Someone taking care of elderly parents stays up until 2 A.M. and gets up at 6 A.M. He or she bathes, dresses, and feeds the parent, then rushes to work, groggy and worn out.

Overall Tax Incentives and LTCI[2]

The Health Insurance Portability and Accountability Act provides several tax incentives (subject to certain conditions and limitations) to purchasers of private LTCI.

1. LTC insurance premiums are deductible as a medical expense, for those who itemize their deductions.
2. LTC insurance benefits received by a claimant are tax-free to the recipient.
3. LTC expenses not covered are tax-deductible.
4. Employers who pay LTC insurance premiums on behalf of an employee can deduct that premium as a business expense, as they do for medical insurance.
5. LTC insurance premiums paid by an employer on behalf of an employee are not treated as income to that employee.

Sample Quotes

Get familiar with the information in Tables 2.1 and 2.2 and Figure 2.2. They will enable you to select the long-term care and long-term care insurance appropriate for you and your loved ones.

- LTCI Quotes.
- Long-Term Care Insurance Questionnaire.

How to Read the Tables

As you can see from Table 2.1, a 45-year-old man who has a benefit period of four years with 60 days elimination would be paying $447 a year. His wife, Mrs. Valued Client (Table 2.2), with the same benefit period—four years, with 60 days elimination—

Table 2.1
Sample LTCI Quotes (Client's Age: 45-Year-Old Man)

LTC Benefit: $150 Daily[a]
Name: Mr. Valued Client
Age: 45

Elimination Period	2 yrs	3 yrs	4 yrs	5 yrs	6 yrs	10 yrs	Unlimited
30 days	$335	$396	$487	$548	$579	$640	$700
60 days	$307	$363	$447	$503	$530	$586	$642
90 days	$279	$330	$406	$457	$482	$533	$584
180 days	$251	$297	$365	$411	$434	$480	$525
365 days	$223	$264	$325	$365	$386	$426	$467

Benefit Period applies across 2 yrs–Unlimited columns.

[a]No guaranteed rates are implied. Rates may change with age, health condition, or year of application.

would be paying $427 a year. ($447 + $427 = $874 a year, or approximately $73 a month for both.)

I stress this because one of the reasons folks reject LTCI at the outset is they think it's outrageously expensive. However, $73 a month with a major insurance company, in exchange for a $300 daily benefit, is not bad. This is a daily benefit *for husband and wife.* A $300 daily benefit for four years translates into a total benefit of $432,000. This level of protection, for $73 a month, makes sense. That's why I said earlier: You cannot afford not to own it.

Table 2.2
Sample LTCI Quotes (Client's Age: 42-Year-Old Woman)

LTC Benefit with Yearly Premium Quoted
Name: Mrs. Valued Client
Age: 42

Elimination Period	2 yrs	3 yrs	4 yrs	5 yrs	6 yrs	10 yrs	Unlimited
30 days	$305	$376	$467	$518	$548	$609	$670
60 days	$279	$343	$427	$475	$503	$558	$614
90 days	$254	$310	$386	$431	$457	$508	$558
180 days	$228	$277	$345	$388	$411	$457	$503
365 days	$203	$244	$305	$345	$365	$406	$447

$150 Daily Benefit Period applies across 2 yrs–Unlimited columns.

Please fill out this form as completely as possible.

Member Name:		Spouse:	
Date of Birth:		Date of Birth:	
Daytime Phone: ( ) -		Evening Phone: ( ) -	
Best Time to Call: _____AM/PM			
Height:	Weight:	Height:	Weight:
Have you used tobacco products in the last 5 years? YES NO		Have you used tobacco products in the last 5 years? YES NO	
Date of last complete physical exam:		Date of last complete physical exam:	
Have you been hospitalized in the last 5 years? YES NO		Have you been hospitalized in the last 5 years? YES NO	
What was the reason for the hospital visit?		What was the reason for the hospital visit?	
Are you taking prescription medications? YES NO		Are you taking prescription medications? YES NO	
Name of Medication	Dosage	Condition Taken for	Name of Medication	Dosage	Condition Taken for

Figure 2.2   Sample LTCI Medical Questionnaire

LTCI Questionnaire

Figure 2.2 shows a standard document that many companies use. They will ask you to complete this questionnaire before the application process. Think of it as an entrance or prescreening questionnaire. By filling out this questionnaire correctly and accurately, the company can probably give you an accurate quote on the proposed cost of your long-term care insurance.

LTCI Application

What to Look for in a Quality Policy   Shopping for long-term care may seem like a daunting task, but it shouldn't be. You may find yourself bombarded with unfamiliar terms as you review various plans. Here are key terms to keep in mind and what you ought to expect from a quality policy.

Benefit Period   A policy should provide sufficient coverage for an extended stay, usually with a minimum coverage of three to four years. With a lifetime benefit period, there would be no limit on the time over which benefits are paid. The longer the benefit period, the higher your premium will be.

Daily Benefit Amount   You should choose an affordable daily benefit, so you don't have to use your assets to pay for LTCI. Our guideline for a daily benefit amount is 100 percent of the prevailing nursing home cost in your area. The amount of coverage you choose may vary, based on the amount of income you have available to pay for LTC expenses. The higher the daily benefit amount you select, the higher your premium.

Home Health Care   Most people prefer to receive care at home for the longest possible time. In some situations, proper home health care coverage can delay or even eliminate the need for nursing home care. The daily benefit amount and the length of the benefit period you select for home health care will affect your premium. Most policies integrate home health care into the core policy, and you can choose a home health care benefit that is 50 percent to 100 percent of the nursing home benefit.

For some policies, home health care coverage is available through a rider to the policy. Adult day care is generally included as part of home health care coverage. Assisted living—which generally involves a less intensive level of care than what is provided in a nursing home—may be a part of either the nursing home or home health care provisions, depending upon the policy.

Inflation Protection   It is important that policy benefits keep pace with increasing nursing home and home health care costs. To protect against inflation, you may want to purchase a policy that includes an automatic inflation provision, where premiums stay level while your daily benefit increases at 5 percent each year. This additional protection is recommended to those 74 years of age and younger.

For those 75 and older—depending upon the insurance company selected—it may be more cost effective to choose a higher daily benefit without the inflation protection option. Be cautious about policies offering inflation protection by permitting you to buy additional coverage every one, two, or three years. By the time you reach the point when you require care, the premiums for this additional coverage may have risen to the point where they are no longer affordable.

Elimination Period (Deductible or Waiting Period)   The elimination period choices vary from one policy to the next—generally from 0 to 100 days. The longer the elimination period, the lower your premium will be. Following is an example of how the elimination period works. If you were to choose an elimination period of 20 days, you would receive no benefits and would have to pay the nursing home costs from other resources for the first 20 days. On the twenty-first day, the insurance company starts paying the cost of your care, up to the daily benefit amount you selected.

Financially Stable Company   It is important to choose an insurance company that will pay benefits when you need them. A.M. Best, Fitch, Standard & Poor's, and Moody's are companies that specialize in evaluating the financial condition of life and health insurance companies. While no one can provide any guarantees, we recommend that you choose an insurance company that recently received high ratings from at least two of those rating services and that you review the rating hierarchy.

Guaranteed Renewable   As long as the premium for a guaranteed renewable policy is paid on time, the insurance company must renew the policy annually, even if the insured's health has deteriorated. Premiums will generally remain at the level stated in your policy for the life of the policy, and can change only if the state insurance commissioner approves the change for everyone who has the same policy from the same company in your state.

No Prior Hospital Stay Is Required   Unlike Medicare, you do not need a prior hospitalization to be eligible for benefits. This is particularly important since only half the people entering nursing homes received care in a hospital first. Rather, many people are admitted to an LTC facility following a period of care at home. There are two ways to qualify for policy benefits: (1) Your physician certifies that you require help with activities such as eating, bathing, dressing, mobility, toileting, or continence; and (2) You are physically able to perform the activities of daily living, but you need to be reminded to do so because of organically based dementia such as Alzheimer's disease.

No Requirement for Skilled Care in a Nursing Home before Benefits Are Paid   There are three levels of care provided in a nursing home: skilled, intermediate, and custodial. It is important your LTCI policy pay benefits no matter what level of care you or your loved one requires.

Home Health Care that Does Not Require Confinement in a Nursing Home   If you purchase a policy that includes coverage for home health care, the policy should stipulate that home health care benefits will be paid without your loved one having to enter a nursing home first. Many people require home health care assistance, not nursing home care, after leaving a hospital. People often enter a nursing home only after home health care arrangements have become unsuitable or insufficient.

Waiver of Premium Benefit   Under policies that include this benefit, after you pay nursing home benefits for a defined period (generally 90 consecutive days), premiums that would otherwise be due under the policy are waived. For most policies, the waiver applies to both nursing home and home health care.

Return of Premium Benefit   Ask your agent if the policy under review is one that will return your premium if the benefits are not used. If this benefit is included, it most likely means that the premiums now will cost more than they otherwise would—but ask anyway.

Covers Alzheimer's Disease and Senile Dementia   The LTC policy must provide nursing home and home health care benefits for those suffering from these illnesses. How do you know which

coverage you should choose or which company you should select? Evaluate the information you received based on your particular needs.

An insurance or financial professional who understands LTC
can help you properly evaluate your needs by comparing several
different carriers and the policies they offer. When appropriate,
this professional can work with you, your family, and financial or
legal advisors to help obtain effective insurance protection at an
affordable premium.

Payment History   Generally, the literature from a company will
not go into detail on their payment history, and that's okay. A
quick call to your state's insurance department will verify how
quickly XYZ Insurance Company pays its long-term care claims.
You'll discover that insurance companies are generally swift in
paying their long-term care claims, because they want to maintain their status as ethical and service-oriented companies.

In addition, insurance companies not only look out for their
customers, but they *do look out for each other.* They know that if
XYZ Company defaults and goes out of business, or it delays its
rightful payment to owners, that's a black eye on all insurance
companies and the insurance industry as a whole. They will not
let that happen.

Also, insurance regulators are tight and demanding. They
keep "feet to the fire" on the insurance companies operating in
their respective states. When necessary, they will either guarantee
or facilitate the payment of long-term care claims.

What If It's Too Late?

You're stuck now—no long-term care insurance. Let's start going
through insurance papers, checkbooks, bank statements, file

folders, desk drawers, deposit boxes, and will (or trust) documents. What can we find?

If you're not sure, answer the following questions:

- Do you or your loved one have a lot of money lying around?
- Do you or your loved one have life insurance with abundant cash values?
- Do you or your loved one have critical-illness insurance?
- Do you or your loved one have a lot of equity in your home? Are you or your parents candidates for a reverse mortgage?
- Do you or your parents have one of those annuities that pays for long-term care?
- Are you or your loved ones eligible for VA benefits?
- Is your loved one eligible for hospice care?

Here are your options if it's too late for a long-term care policy.

A Reverse Mortgage: Your Guaranteed Home Equity Income Program

There have been so many questions about using reverse mortgages for a variety of senior needs that I've included this lengthy section. I should add that it is not necessary to wait until an urgent need arises for long-term care to tap the money from a reverse mortgage. For many seniors, it makes sense to tap the assets in a reverse mortgage in order to get money anytime to pay for LTC premiums. A *small* portion of the reverse mortgage money can pay for long-term care insurance premiums now, which is smarter than using a big portion to pay for long-term care later.

I have a client—let's call her Mary—who's 79 years old. She took out a reverse mortgage on her house and received $100,000 cash. We put that $100,000 in a guaranteed income account paying her approximately $823 a month. That's about a $9\frac{1}{2}$ percent fixed and guaranteed return. With that $823, she has dedicated $195 a month to buying long-term care insurance, so that when the time comes for home health care, or assisted living, or a nursing home, she will have the money to pay for it.

This is a much smarter strategy than waiting until the long-term care crisis comes and then taking the entire $100,000 to pay for home health care or assisted living and long-term care. Incidentally, when Mary dies, this income will continue to her beneficiaries, so she will have an estate to pass on as well as having protection for her long-term care needs.

Reverse mortgages aren't for everyone. One size does not fit all. Any investment or financial decision demands suitability. Make sure the investment or financial decision is suitable *for you.* Talk to an independent financial consultant who can shop several mortgage lenders for you and help you determine suitability. Not sure what this means? Here's a rundown of frequently asked questions on this alternative option to long-term care insurance.

What exactly is a reverse mortgage? As the name implies, you are getting money *from* the mortgage company rather than giving money *to* the mortgage company. This is a reverse of what you did all your life. Let's say your home is valued at $200,000, and let's say that the value of your home, or your loved one's home, is $200,000. Your loved one is 72 years old. The lender says that she can get $150,000. She gets a check for $150,000. She can use that check for whatever she wants. In our example, you may need the money for long-term health care expenses.

You should know the four irreversible "nevers" on reverse mortgages:

1. You never give up title.
2. The amount of the reverse mortgage will never be more than the sale price of the home.

3. You'll never be forced to move. You retain title ownership of the home as long as it is your primary residence.
4. You never make a payment.

Am I a candidate for a reverse mortgage? Yes, if

- You are age 62 or older.
- You occupy your home as your primary residence.
- You own the home free and clear, or you have an existing mortgage balance large enough to justify a reverse mortgage.
- You're seeking tax-free funds that never have to be repaid.
- You have difficulty meeting health need or retirement need expenses.

How are the funds paid out to me? When you take out a reverse mortgage, the money is paid to you in three different ways. You can receive: (1) A single lump sum, which I recommend because, in a guaranteed growth-and-income fund, it gives you security, privacy, control, flexibility, and the safety of diversity; (2) You can have a certain amount sent to you every month; or (3) You can simply take out a line of credit that lets you use the money whenever you want to.

The bottom line is that a reverse mortgage turns the value of your home into cash right now, which you can use to help fix up your home, pay additional medical expenses, or to help your kids or grandkids.

I have an elderly client who has a son and a daughter-in-law, both of whom are on Social Security disability. They've been living in an apartment and barely making it. My client converted her $225,000 Dallas home into $160,000 in cash through a reverse mortgage. With that, she helped her disabled son and disabled daughter-in-law buy a home with all the handicapped features they needed. Additionally, she placed some of the money in a guaranteed income account from which she has been able to pay a monthly premium for a long-term care insurance plan. This LTCI plan means that she will not be financially wiped out when the time comes that she is not able to take care of herself.

The most important thing to remember in taking out a reverse mortgage is that one size does not fit all. Don't make a decision based upon general comments you hear on the radio or television or comments from your friends. Check it out yourself in your area with an independent financial consultant.

I've spoken with a consultant and I'm going for it—now what? After the closing, you have up to three days to cancel the transaction. It's not irrevocable. (Saturday, by the way, counts as a business day.) So, you have plenty of time for your family, attorney, or CPA to look at it. By the way, if the person or company who's helping you with the reverse mortgage is doing it right, they will insist that you bring in other family members before you close on the reverse mortgage. This doesn't mean that they need the approval of other family members (it's your home, your money), but they want to be sure nothing backfires.

Reverse mortgages are suitable for some, particularly for seniors who are home rich but cash poor, and who otherwise couldn't afford to pay for long-term care or long-term care insurance. They may not be suitable for someone who's on Medicaid, SSI, or other programs for low-income seniors. Check with your independent financial consultant to see if the proceeds from reverse mortgages would potentially interfere with Medicaid, SSI, or other payments.

Some people dismiss the idea of reverse mortgage outright because they think a better way for them to raise money is to simply sell the home to their children and then rent it back from them. Bad idea. There can be tax problems, inheritance problems, and most of all, while things may be going well for you now, what if . . .

You don't want to be held captive by somebody else, no matter who it is. You don't want to be living in a rented house where you could be kicked out, especially by a family member.

For a list of lenders in your area who offer reverse mortgages, you can call 866-264-4466 or go to www.reversemortgage.org and click on Find a Lender.

Do You Qualify for VA Benefits?

Of course we do. Mom, Dad, me—we're all vets. Not so fast. Long-term care benefits for vets are not a slam-dunk. There are 24 million vets. The Veteran's Administration meets the LTC needs of only about 20 percent, and those are primarily the poor and disabled.

More vets are getting older, leading to an increased demand for long-term care. The VA facilities around the nation are over-burdened, understaffed, and underfunded. There's a priority system for all VA health care and especially VA long-term care recipients. Those who have a service-oriented disability or who are broke get the LTC care first. Are you in that category? If not, then VA care is not a solution for you.

Do You Have Critical Illness Insurance?

Critical illness insurance pays a lump sum upon diagnosis of one of a dozen or so diseases or injuries, for people who need help with three or more activities of daily living and require permanent daily supervision, as diagnosed by a Board-certified neurologist. Critical illness (CI) insurance also covers multiple sclerosis, heart attack, stroke, life threatening cancer, organ transplants, paralysis, kidney failure requiring dialysis, blindness, deafness, or severe burns.

Lump sums under this plan can be anywhere from $25,000 to $1 million. The lump sum benefit of a critical illness policy can cover miscellaneous expenses covered through major illness, such as: insurance deductibles and co-pays; and travel expenses, such as meals, lodging, and airfare to seek additional medical treatment.

That could be money you use for yourself or for a loved one. CI insurance also covers experimental treatment and/or drugs; treatment outside of a managed care network; child care; elder care; salary replacement for time away from work; household help like cooking, cleaning, and laundry; home modifications; mortgage payments; and other debts.

Is CI insurance a replacement for LTCI? Absolutely not! Access to benefits is tougher, as even Alzheimer's patients would have to need help with at least three activities. Long-term care insurance requires help with only two ADLs, and there is no ADL requirement at all for Alzheimer's patients under long-term care.

The critical illness benefit is a lump sum cash benefit, which can bring a strong temptation to spend it for things other than long-term care. You still may need ongoing long-term care expenses now or later, so don't consider it as a substitute for long-term care insurance. Moreover, a lump sum cash benefit may be difficult to budget so that it lasts throughout a long-term care condition.

Another disadvantage to critical illness insurance is that benefits are reduced at age 65 and up, when you most need protection. On the other hand, your long-term care insurance endures indefinitely, unless you put a time limit on it.

Do You Have an Accelerated Death Benefit (ADB) Life Insurance Policy?

This is a life insurance policy that provides cash advances against all or part of the death benefit, if used for long-term care expenses while the insured is still living. Check to see if your parents, or your loved one, has one of these ADB policies.

Typically, if the *death benefit* is $200,000, for example, you can access two percent a month for nursing home care, or one percent for home health care. Therefore, on a $200,000 policy, that would be $4,000 *a month* that could be accessed for nursing home care, or $2,000 a month for home health care. Of course, this doesn't go on indefinitely. If the cost of the long-term care or home health care becomes excessive and exceeds the death benefit amount, then those payments stop.

Clearly, there are three downsides to this type of policy and this type of payment plan: (1) the money will eventually run out; (2) there is no built-in inflation protection. In our example, you're going to get a flat $4,000 a month, and that's it; and (3) it may destroy the purpose that you bought the policy to begin with. If you bought that to leave an estate to your spouse or to your children or to a charity, then early withdrawals for LTC smash your original goal.

This accelerated death benefit is a non-death benefit. You don't have to die to get it. Check your ADB policy and see if it has a waiver of premium notice, meaning that if the owner becomes disabled or terminally ill, he or she doesn't have to pay the premium any longer. He or she might also have a standard whole life or universal life policy with an ADB rider. This rider could provide the benefits just described. Check all policies carefully.

Do You Qualify for a Viatical Settlement?

You've got a terminal disease, and you know you're going to die in two to three years. Your medical expenses in the next two to three years will be astronomical. You could go on welfare (Medicaid), but you won't be able to stay at home, as you wanted. How do you come up with the money to be able to pay for extended home health care?

Solution: "Hey," you say, "I've got this life insurance policy with this $200,000 death benefit. I want to sell it to you for $120,000. So when I die, you'll get the full $200,000. You give me the $120,000 now, and I'll make you the Owner and Beneficiary of this policy. I'm the insured, and I'm going to die soon, and since I'm considered disabled and/or terminally ill, there are no more premiums to pay. You just hold on to this policy until I die, and you'll get $200,000."

By the way, if the Insured does die in two to three years, that will be about a 20 percent annual return for the Owner of this policy. That, in essence, is what a viatical settlement (or a viatical policy) is. The word "viatical" comes from Vatican, which refers to the supplies needed to perform the last rites for Roman soldiers who were sent into battle—and who were expected to die. Well, the idea here is that the viatical settlement provides financial supplies for the afflicted during their final journey toward death.

See if your loved one has an insurance policy with a sizeable death benefit. If so, check with your independent financial consultant, who should know how to access a viatical settlement in your state. If not, you can call the state insurance department. If done right, the viatical settlement you receive is tax-free. Be sure to check with your local tax advisor.

Actual case: A 52-year-old man is diagnosed with lymphatic cancer. His life expectancy is 24 to 30 months. He has a cash value life insurance policy with a death benefit of $245,000. His accumulated cash value is $10,500. The surrender cash value is only $4,500. Instead of keeping the policy in force and paying premiums, or surrendering it for a mere $4,500, he chooses to sell the policy to a viatical company for $160,000. He uses the money then to take his family on a fall foliage trip to New England, to modify his home to make it more comfortable and more usable during his illness, and to hire a live-in home health care aide.

Do You Have a Life Settlement Policy?

Remember, a viatical is for someone who's been declared terminally ill. A life settlement is available for older people who are not ill. You sell your policy to a life settlement company and you use the money for a variety of things. In addition to long-term care, you make cash gifts to family members, purchase interest in a business, fund the purchase of long-term care insurance for a spouse, and so on. This is ideal for someone who doesn't need the lump sum amount from the insurance policy anymore. Something has changed in your life, and you no longer need that lump sum for college tuition or a spouse's income. There's been a change in your estate size, due to the sale of a business or a settlement from a divorce, so you sell your policy.

For example, I have an 82-year-old client with health concerns. He's had a $300,000 universal life policy. Making those premium payments on that policy was becoming a financial burden, and he was concerned about long-term care. He didn't qualify for long-term care because of health problems. A life settlement gave him $125,000. Selling the policy relieved this client and his wife of monthly premium payments, enabled him to purchase a long-term care policy for his wife, and provide funds for his own long-term care needs.

Here's the unique value of a life settlement policy. Many times, a senior will drop life insurance because it is not needed or the premium is too expensive. There is no need to drop it. Sell it instead! Life settlements can be a great option and great benefit for those who need money for long-term care, including home health care.

Do You Own a Single-Premium, Long-Term Care Policy?

You or your loved one some years ago put down a lump sum, single premium on a life insurance policy: $50,000, $100,000, and $200,000—whatever. You have an immediate death benefit to pass on to your estate. However, double the amount of your deposit is immediately available for long-term care, so if you put down $100,000, you have $200,000 available now to help with long-term care expenses.

Do You Own a Long-Term Care Annuity?

This allows you to access money immediately from your annuity, without surrender charges, for long-term care. A physician must certify that you need assistance with two of the six Activities of Daily Living: bathing, continence, dressing, eating, transporting, and toileting (or you are cognitively impaired). When you show you can't perform two, then you can access money from this long-term care annuity.

Do You Own an Immediate Annuity, Sometimes Called an Income Annuity?

You put a lump sum in, and it pays you a guaranteed monthly income check. The older you are, the bigger the check is. You can even set it up where you can have a beneficiary receive the balance of the money. For example, at this writing, an 89-year-old female who clearly has some type of debilitating illness or injury could deposit approximately $150,000 and receive $5,000 a month. That's guaranteed for life. If she puts that money in a traditional CD or a traditional fixed annuity, she would not be able to get anywhere near that amount. An immediate annuity is designed for someone who needs abundant and guaranteed cash flow—now.

These are called SPIAs: single-premium income annuity. These annuities guarantee a series of payments over a specified time. There's also a version of these called medically-underwritten annuities. If you show—in addition to needing long-term care—that you suffer from a medical condition that shortens your lifespan, you can get a bigger annuity income payout than one just based on your age.

One benefit of owning an annuity that has a long-term care benefit attached to it is that if you're uninsurable, the annuity may be the way to go. Some policies allow you to put in a lump-sum payment. That lump-sum payment does three things: (1) If the policy is left alone, it can grow as a high-yielding tax-deferred CD; (2) You can access money from it for long-term care any time; and (3) If you don't access the money, then your beneficiary will get the death benefit from it

If you do access the money for long-term care, there may still be money available to pass on to beneficiaries, but of course, those monies will be subtracted from the death benefit.

Do You Own a Combination Long-Term Care Policy?

You're 65 years old, and you've got $200,000 in the bank. It's your safe money, your rainy day money. You plan on never touching it, but you want it available just in case. You plan to leave it to your kids, grandkids, or favorite charity after you die. So you put the $200,000 in a combination LTC policy. Why would you do this?

Because you could potentially double the amount that you leave to your kids or your grandkids, *or* have guaranteed long-term care protection.

You see, with this strategy, you've taken out two long-term care riders within the policy. The first will pay monthly until the total death benefit, limited to 2 percent of the current death benefit per month for 50 months. That obviously would be $4,000 a month for 50 months. If you needed long-term care that exceeded that amount, your second rider is paying the benefit for another 50 months, meaning that the total long-term care benefit is 100 months (50 months plus 50 months equals 100 months). You can also get it with a lifetime option.

So here's what you've done. You've enhanced the amount to be left to your heirs if you don't need care, or you've created a whole pile of money just for long-term care. This pile gives you more private pay options. The downside of this is that it is medically underwritten, so you've got to be healthy enough for this combination of a long-term care policy and a life insurance policy.

Do You Own a Universal or Whole Life Policy?

The potential benefits of this type of policy are: (1) You can get a dividend-paid-out option. If you have this, the insurer will give you the dividends on the policy; (2) You can cash in the policy completely to receive the surrender cash value. This could keep the policy intact, but in some cases, minus the cash value; (3) You can take out a policy loan against the cash value of the life insurance; and (4) You can withdraw from the cash value of the policy. This is called "surrendering."

None of these alternatives are intended to be substitutes for long-term care. We mention these alternatives only if it's too late. If there is time to buy long-term care insurance, buy it!

Remember the AARP proverb: "Living without long-term care insurance is like driving without car insurance."

CHAPTER SUMMARY

A life insurance policy has a variety of ways to provide cash to pay for long-term care insurance or long-term health care. Since many people who need long-term care are not terminally ill, it is not necessary in those cases to count on products that have a terminally ill requirement, for example, viaticals and accelerated death benefits.

If you cash in life insurance for long-term care, remember that the death benefit is no longer available to your beneficiaries. As with any long-term care funding options, check with your local legal, financial, and tax person regarding your options.

ACTION STEPS

- ❏ Admit that you aren't invincible and get yourself, your spouse, *and* your parents a long-term insurance policy.
- ❏ Be sure to carefully review every page of your long-term insurance policy before signing on the dotted line.
- ❏ Ask your policy provider detailed questions so you won't miss the fine print of any policy you decide to purchase. Don't be embarrassed to ask questions if there are terms in the policy that you're not familiar with!
- ❏ Before you stop paying premiums and discontinuing any life insurance contracts, check with your independent financial planner to see if your policy can be sold.
- ❏ If you don't qualify for long-term care, be proactive and explore the other avenues discussed in this chapter (e.g., immediate annuity, viatical settlement, VA benefits, etc.).

CONCLUSION

Don't swoon into the sleep of "Not me . . . it'll never happen to me. I'll never need long-term care." Rather, *wake up*!

Do all you can to ensure that you and your loved ones are protected financially. Don't wait until the last minute or think it can't happen to you. Otherwise, you or your loved one may spend your final days financially and physically spent.

And the best remedy to keep yourself from between a rock and a hard place is prevention.

CHAPTER 3

The Prevention:
How to Make It to 98 and
Love and Live Every Minute

Growing old is inevitable; feeling old is a choice.

To preserve health is a moral and religious duty, for health is the basis of all social virtues. We can no longer be useful when not well.
— Dr. Samuel Johnson, father of dictionaries

THIS CHAPTER DEALS WITH THE PHYSICAL, EMOTIONAL, INTELLECTUAL, and spiritual dynamics of aging. The *physical* strategies mentioned later in this chapter come from my radio colleague, Dr. Ken Cooper, the father of American fitness, author of *Aerobics*, President/CEO of the Cooper Fitness Center in Dallas, and personal physician to George W. Bush. Combined, these strategies helped thousands to stay *out* of nursing homes . . . and enjoy their final days at home.

And by the way, how long will it be until you are facing your final days at home? How long do you plan to live? Take this test.

Instructions: Start with 87 years (the average life expectancy of a person living in an industrialized nation). Depending on your answers to the following questions, add or subtract the appropriate number of years.

ATTITUDE: Are you optimistic? Do you generally approach life with good humor? Are you able to let go of things that are stressful?

   If no, subtract five years.   _____

EXERCISE: Do you set aside at least 30 minutes a day, 3 days a week to exercise? Muscle-building exercises are particularly important.

   If no, subtract five years.   _____

GENES: Do you have at least some family members who have lived into their 90s or later? Exceptional longevity runs strongly in families.

   If yes, add 10 years.   _____

INTERESTS: Do you do things that are challenging to your brain regularly? It's important to take on activities that are novel and complex.

   If yes, add five years.   _____

NUTRITION: Do you have a diet that keeps you lean? Carrying extra weight is not conducive to longevity.

   If no, subtract seven years.   _____

SMOKING: Do you smoke?

   If yes, subtract five years.   _____

   TOTAL   _____

Many have scored 100+ on this test. Are you one of them? Would you like to be?

Verona Johnston, Age 114

If you take some cues from this simple test, you could give Verona Johnston a run for her money. At 114 years of age, she was the oldest American alive. Johnston, a retired Latin teacher, mother of four, grandmother of 13, and great-grandmother of 23, turned 114 on August 6, 2004, making her the oldest documented person in the United States. Johnston lived on her own until age 98. She shared a house in Worthington, Ohio, with her daughter Julie Johnson, 81, and Julie's husband Bruce, 83, until her death in December 2004.

Johnston's mind was so sharp that she still solved word jumbles in her head; remembered joke punch lines; and when she couldn't sleep at night, ran through the names of her 36 grandchildren and great-grandchildren, rather than counting sheep.

Granted, her vision was nearly gone, so she gave up playing bridge at 110. She no longer traveled to visit family in Omaha, Nebraska, and San Diego alone, as she did at 100; and she relied on a walking cane, but Johnston could still hear fairly well, and she loved listening to books on tape.

Johnston's attitude may have played a critical role in her longevity. She didn't dwell on what age had taken away from her. And good genes and a whopping dose of good luck didn't hurt, either. Johnston's father died at 69 and her mother at 85. Her younger sister Vern died in 1997 at 105. Although Johnston had surgery for breast cancer in her nineties and a heart attack so minor she never noticed it, she had generally enjoyed great health.

Johnston had no special diet, but she had always been big on moderation. Her daily snack consisted of orange juice and exactly one cracker, one cinnamon-drop candy, and one cashew.

Johnston, a graduate of Drake University in 1912, never smoked. This churchgoing minister's daughter never touched alcohol, either, until she moved in with her daughter and son-in-law, who introduced her to Bailey's Irish Cream, which became part of an occasional family happy hour. As far as exercise went, she simply wove it into her active schedule. She climbed up and down seven flights of stairs to her old apartment well into her nineties.

Seiryu Toguchi, Age 103

Sciryu Toguchi of Okinawa rises at 6 A.M., in the house where he was born. Every morning, he opens the shutters to signal to his neighbors that he is still alive. He eats breakfast after completing stretching exercises along with a radio broadcast: whole-grain rice and miso soup with vegetables. He picks weeds for two hours in his 1,000-square-foot field, whose crops are "goya"—a variety of bitter gourd—a reddish-purple sweet potato called "imo," and okra. With the profits from his produce, Toguchi buys rice and meat.

Since his wife Kame passed seven years ago at 93, he does all the housework himself. His appreciation of his freedom led him to reject his children's suggestion to come live with them. His doctors insist Toguchi is in excellent health, but he takes no chances. He goes to the hospital right away if he feels that something is wrong, according to his daughter Sumiko Sakhara, 74.

Toguchi eats lunch at 12:30 that consists of goya stir-fry with egg and tofu. He takes a nap for about an hour, then goes back to the field for two more hours. After dinner, he caters to his musical inclinations by playing traditional songs on his three-stringed *sanshin*. He also makes an entry in his diary, which he has done every night for the past decade. For a nightcap, he may take a sip of the wine he makes from aloe, garlic, and turmeric.

Jack LaLanne, Age 91

And what about that ubiquitous youngster, Jack LaLanne, age 91? Do you remember Jack? He probably affected you like he affected me. He grabbed my attention on the TV screen. "Don't you want to look your best? Wouldn't you like to feel great all the time and have more energy? Well, you can! All you need to do is eat right and exercise and you'll feel like a million dollars!"

Like a faithful soldier, I was inducted into the world of *The Jack LaLanne Show*. Five days a week, sit-ups, jumping jacks, and side bends became routine. Celery and carrots became my band of brothers. I felt his enthusiasm. I followed his directions. I'd stretch my right fingers to my left toes or sit on the couch to pull my knees toward my chest and extend, or hold onto a chair for balance as I'd lift a leg skyward. His commands inspired me.

I learned that success came hard for Francois Henri LaLanne. He overcame severe obstacles: conquering family inhibitions, first-generation challenges in America, and rejection by his older brother. He conquered a 15-year-long maternal bribe to soothe his constant anxiety: sucking on a homemade pacifier, a towel soaked in cornstarch, sugar, and water. He remembers his wretched childhood in Bakersfield, California, as producing a "sugarholic who was irritable, weak, and skinny." With rotting teeth, he faced boy and girl bullies alike. As the runt, he got picked on—so much so that he had suicidal thoughts.

Through a compassionate neighbor's intervention, the depressed, bashful kid found his savior. A nutrition teacher, Paul Bragg, promised new life to a desperate Francois. "He told me I could get out of my misery, and I believed him." Within two days, Jack LaLanne was born. The teenager took control, with no more headaches, boils, or negative thinking. He began training at his local YMCA gym.

During the next seven decades, he kept stretching, training, teaching, encouraging, and eating right. "And you wonder why I'm enthusiastic?" he asks.

So what steps can you take to ensure that *you* live well in your golden years like Jack LaLanne? The following pages include health-related studies in the news that give us a good clue to how to live to 98 and love and live every moment.

Health Studies: Good Habits Pay Off for the Elderly

In an article published in *The Dallas Morning News*, by Associated Press writer Lindsey Tanner, we are reminded that regular walking has numerous benefits, such as helping to prevent mental decline and Alzheimer's disease, a finding substantiated by studies conducted among patients 70 and older.

In addition to walking, taking Mom's advice to heart and eating your vegetables is also a good habit to develop. One of the studies on longevity was conducted among Europeans ages 70 to 90, who ate a Mediterranean-style diet rich in fruits, vegetables, fish, and olive oil. The findings of the study indicated that these individuals had a 23 percent lower risk of death during a 10-year follow-up than those with less healthy eating habits.

Moreover, the study found a 65 percent lower mortality risk among those who combined the Mediterranean-style diet with three other healthy habits: moderate alcohol use, no smoking, and half an hour or more per day of physical activity, including walking.

One of the published exercise studies involved 2,257 retired men in Hawaii, who ranged in age from 71 to 93. Those who walked less than a quarter-mile a day were nearly twice as likely to develop Alzheimer's or other forms of dementia as men who walked more than two miles everyday.

Also, one of the studies conducted involved 16,466 female nurses ages 70 to 81. This study found that even women who walked leisurely 1½ hours a week did better on tests of mental function than less active women.

The *Journal of the American Medical Association* published the studies in their September 2004 issue.

It is important to keep in mind that though the studies involved older patients, they don't clearly tell us whether adopting healthy habits late in life will have the same benefits as a lifetime of healthy behavior, since participants weren't asked how long they'd engaged in the activities. So start today!

The sections that follow provide you with helpful strategies to success in the four key areas of aging: physical, emotional, intellectual, and spiritual.

Physical

- *Get a thorough checkup every year.* You don't just run into the corner family care clinic to give blood and urine and take BP and a temp. You make one of those all-day appointments at least once a year: bone density, stress test, eyes, ears, fat ratio test, ultrasounds, body scan, and so on.
- *Run for your life* (after consulting your doctor, that is). Running is very therapeutic because it releases endorphins, which are nature's natural heroin. Endorphins give you a positive high. Running cleanses your mind as well as your emotions. Thousands of runners testify to the fact that when feeling overwhelmed by problems, going out and doing a few laps gives them a fresh perspective.
- *Eat the right foods.* You know the drill, five servings of fruits and vegetables, low salt and fat—which seems to work for the 600 inhabitants in Okinawa who are 100 years old or more. Their diets are simple: low in salt and fat and high in

fruits and vegetables, packed with fiber and antioxidant sub-
stances that protect against cancer, heart disease, and
stroke. They have a much lower incidence of dementia,
Alzheimer's, or other forms of mental disease.

- *Eat less.* Dr. David Sinclair of Harvard University says that re-
stricting calorie intake could slow down the aging process.
"Evidence for that surprising phenomenon," he says,
"emerged in the 1930s when scientists learned that rats
whose food intake was reduced lived up to 40 percent
longer than their well-fed counterparts."[1] In short, a calorie
reduction strategy is your own "anti-aging pill."

- *Be accountable for your eating habits.* Never blame your poor
health on parents or genes. Don't accept the fatalistic
cliché, "Doesn't matter what I eat. I just look at food and get
fat. I've got bad genes." Studies by Swedish scientists in the
late 1990s, and later confirmed by additional studies, examined pairs of identical twins separated at birth and found
that these sets of twins died at significantly different ages depending upon their lifestyles, eating habits, exercise, and
joie de vivre.

- *Make fasting a part of your diet.* Of course, the ultimate in
eating less is not eating at all, or the practice of fasting.
Fasting does not mean starvation. There are partial fasts,
liquid fasts, juice fasts, water fasts, and there are total and
complete fasts. Check with your doctor to see what's suitable for you.

- *Take proper food supplements.* Read the labels! Don't just get junk
that's loaded with fillers. Read the labels for purity and guarantees. Personally, I like Cooper Complete. These multivita-
mins were shown to lower the oxidation rate of LDL ("bad")
cholesterol. They were also shown to reduce C-reactive pro-
tein (CRP) levels. Consistently high levels of CRP are directly
linked to heart disease and stroke.

- *Chugalug, chugalug, chugalug* . . . water, that is. Drinking *at least* eight cups a day *is not* an option. Because 55 percent to 75 percent of our bodies are made of water, it's important to replenish whatever amount lost throughout the day through sweat and other activities.

- *Keep that sexy smile* and take great care of your teeth. When you have healthy teeth and gums, you can eat the foods you need for proper nutrition . . . and the occasional candy apple, if you absolutely can't resist.

- *Lift weights.* After age 40, muscles atrophy 1 percent a year. The good news is: *You can reverse this trend.* You reverse this trend with slow and low weightlifting. Daily. You can do substantial weightlifting with your own body! It's easy, fun, safe, inexpensive . . . and you can do it at home.

- *Rest and recreate.* Read a good book. Go to a soothing music concert. Go to church. Take a walk in the park. Don't watch TV. That is *not* rest and recreation. No matter what you're watching, the very act of watching TV causes a sense of being drugged or depressed.

- *Drive to stay alive.* Wear seatbelts. Drive defensively. Practice FIDO (forget it and drive on). Every day the roads of Miami, Seattle, Boston, Topeka, Nashville, Dallas, or a thousand other places, are filled with nuts boiling with road rage. They cut you off, and you give them the finger. Now they cut you off again and give you a knife! FIDO. Forget It and Drive On.

Do these habits work? Ask Francesca Skelton. Within three years, Francesca lost her brother and mother. Her brother died at 63—tragically young by today's standards. Her mother reached 97, but arthritis made her final years a torture. "I saw myself getting older and being in pain, too," says Skelton. "I want to live a long time, but only if I'm in good health." Skelton reconsidered everything she ever learned about nutrition, fitness, and daily exercise, and she reached a life-changing conclusion: She could live to be 100, and she could get there in great shape and not be afraid of dying in pain and panic.

Today, the 63-year-old Washingtonian grandmother has the figure of someone 20 years younger. At 5 feet 4 inches, Skelton weighs a mere 111 pounds. She rarely gets so much as a cold, and she's dodged the high blood pressure that runs in her family. But to reach this level of health, she made a real sacrifice. Skelton gave up the equivalent of a meal a day—her daily intake is less than 1,600 calories (a typical adult eats around 2,500). Francesca knew that calorie restriction has the effect of slowing the rate at which animals age, so she decided to seek the same results. "It takes a lot of discipline to follow this diet," she says. "But to me, it's worth it."

Skelton's fat-farm eating habits may seem extreme, but her desire for longevity puts her squarely in the mainstream. In a 2001 telephone survey by the Alliance for Aging Research, a nonprofit advocacy group, 63 percent of respondents said they wanted to reach the age of 100. "The desire to live longer and better is built into the human character," says Dr. Robert N. Butler, author of the Pulitzer Prize-winning *Why Survive? Being Old in America.* Thanks to improvements in medicine and nutrition, Butler adds, "The reality has begun to take hold that you can really do something about living longer . . . by eating right and living right."

So let's summarize the facts of physical health: Exercise can be safe and fun. Your heart can grow stronger with exercise even after age 40 and much beyond. Preventing your blood pressure or cholesterol from elevating in your older years is doable. You can prevent your weight from going up in later years. It is possible to increase muscle mass and muscle tone in your senior years. No matter how long you've been smoking, you can always stop. You can increase bone mass and build bone density in your senior years. You can reverse the process of hardening or clogging of the arteries. In short, with good physical health, you can stay out of a nursing home. That's the whole point of this book, the whole point of this chapter.

Here are some key strategies to success in the emotional aspect of aging.

Emotional

- *Build a desire to win.* Desire is fire, and from this day forward, your desire will be, "I'll make today a great day, regardless of what other people say, think, or do."

  Don't criticize, condemn, or complain.
- *Embrace the perspective.* "Old is a clock, age is an attitude, and health is a choice." I told my wife that when we are 95, I will still be chasing her around the bedroom, and when I catch her, I'll remember why I was chasing her!
- *Build strong relationships.* Folks need your wisdom, patience, guidance, and comfort, and you need theirs. Jean-Paul Sartre was wrong, fatally wrong, when he said "Hell is other people." No, hell is you and your bitterness, your isolation, and your suspicion, when you say you don't need other people.
- *Get involved . . . stay involved.* My clients say to me, "Doc, before you retire, get a lot done, because when you retire, you won't have time. You'll be too busy." They know how to get involved and stay involved.
- *Laugh long, loud, and often.* Act childish. Drop the dignified, mature adult façade, and do something that makes you laugh. Laughing lowers your blood pressure, decreases stress, lifts your spirits, and strengthens your immune system.

- *Give and forgive.* "When you hate somebody, they own you." Let it go. It's good for them; it's good for you. Several studies suggest that in the long run, forgiving does actually benefit you. One study reveals that forgiving can decrease levels of anger and hostility, increase feelings of love, and improve physical and mental health (*Psychotherapy*, 1986, vol. 23, no. 4).

- *Stay positive.* In his article "Beyond Loss" (*Readers Digest*, June 2002, pp. 102 following), researcher Laurence Gonzales says that each year approximately 3,600 people get lost in national parks. Those who ultimately survive display three common actions: a positive mental attitude, compassionate activities, (i.e., helping someone else—the other lost person), and building a fire—the fire of heat and light to cook and stay warm, *and* the fire of hope and enthusiasm to stay alive.

- *Take control.* Accept responsibility for good and bad outcomes. Don't whine, make excuses, or blame others. The greatest compliment you can give yourself is to take responsibility for your actions. The greatest compliment you can give someone else is to hold them responsible for their actions.

- *Dump the guilt.* Guilt in the initial stages can be healthy, if it keeps the thwarter from doing illegal, immoral, dangerous, or stupid things. Guilt is to the soul what pain is to the body. It can help stop us from doing things that are shameful or hurtful; however, sometimes people of authority dump guilt on us when there is no cause to. Sometimes we dump guilt on ourselves when there is no cause to.

  The key to dumping guilt is recognizing: (1) No one's perfect, and everyone makes mistakes; (2) what you've got and where you are is plenty good enough to build again; and (3) accept your mistake, learn from it, and go on.

He

By Richard Mullen

He can turn the tides and calm the angry sea,
He alone decides who writes a symphony.
He lights ev'ry star that makes the darkness bright,
He keeps watch all through each long and lonely night.

He still finds the time to hear a child's first prayer,
Saint or sinner calls and always finds him there.
Though it makes Him sad to see the way we live,
He'll always say "I forgive."

He can touch a tree and turn the leaves to gold,
He knows every lie that you and I have told.
Though it makes Him sad to see the way we live,
He'll always say "I forgive."
He forgives.[2]

- *Channel your stress.* Stress is neutral. It's neither good nor bad. Stress simply means the gap between what you want and what you have. If what you want is good, wholesome, and positive, and what you have now is not yet there, *but you're making progress toward it,* this will relieve the stress. If what you want is good, wholesome, and positive, and *you do nothing to make progress toward it,* this causes stress.

  Another word for stress is disappointment. The only way to handle disappointment is to say, "What's the good in this? How am I going to turn this into something good for me and for others?" That keeps stress channeled and productive. To be alive is to have stress.

  I like the story that Dr. Norman Vincent Peale tells about stress and problems. He says, "I hear people say, 'Stress. I've got all this stress. I want to go someplace where there's no stress.' "

When speaking to a group of business executives in New York City, Dr. Peale said, "Since I have been in your majestic city, I have recently found a place where there is no stress. How many of you are concerned with all the stress you have?" (All hands went up.) "I've found this place where there is no stress. As a matter of fact, it's a community just outside the city. They tell me that 24,553 people live there, and none of them have stress. It's called Greenwood Memorial Cemetery.

"To be alive is to have stress," Dr. Peale continued. "You continue to have stress until the day you die. When you're not having stress and when you're not having obstacles, get on your knees and pray, 'Oh Lord, don't you trust me anymore? Give me some good, man-sized, tough problems.'"

- *Talk to yourself.* The two most important conversations you have every day are the one you have with God and the one you have with yourself. Just listen to yourself sometime. Just listen to yourself. Would you talk to somebody else the way you talk to yourself? *That was dumb. You shouldn't have done that. You knew better than that. I'll never get over that. I'll never forgive myself for that. How could I have done something so stupid?* You wouldn't talk to somebody else like that.

  Talk to yourself in positive, uplifting, constructive, solution-oriented ways. Sure, you make mistakes, but then say to yourself, "What good am I going to bring out of this?" or, "Next time I will . . ."

- *Grab a hero.* Find people with traits you admire and model your actions after theirs. When asked how one might reach age 90 happy and healthy, Dr. Norman Vincent Peale said, "Enjoy life! Enjoy God, friends, and your family."

- *Practice Doc's Medicine for Life* (See box.)

Doc's Medicine for Life

✓ *Unexpected help comes from unpredictable sources to the person who remains positive, enthusiastic, and cheerful.* What does that mean? You're God, looking down from heaven. Today, you have talents, blessings, riches, and opportunities to pour into somebody's heart and head. Whom are you going to choose?

Here is Peggy Pessimist: negative, hostile, critical, hateful, unforgiving, and complaining. So, you're God, and you say to yourself, "Why should I waste my talents, blessings, opportunities, and riches on Peggy? She'll waste 'em for sure. She'll say, 'How come I don't have more?' or 'This should have been here sooner,' or 'I don't have enough time to use them.' "

Then you look at Pamela Positive. Pamela Positive is— well, positive, enthusiastic, and cheerful. She counts her blessings. She looks for opportunities to help. She's grateful. She looks for opportunities to improve herself. When she falls down, she gets up. She looks for the best in herself. She looks for the best in others. So, as God, you say to yourself, "If I give blessings, talents, opportunities, and riches to Pamela Positive, she sure enough will use them. Go for it."

✓ *No one knows enough to worry.* What do we do when we choose to worry? When we choose to worry, we choose to pitch our brain into the future while saying, "I know the next five minutes, or the next five days, or five months from now, or a year from now, is going to be b-a-a-d. It's going to be terrible. Things never get better, only worse for me. I know it's going to be bad."

No one knows that! You don't know what's going to happen in the next five minutes, five days, five months, or five years, for that matter. What we do know is this: We cannot predict the future, but we can create it by our moment-to-moment actions.

✓ *Celebrate the now.* On occasion, we foolishly tell ourselves that life will be better after our grades are improved; we move to a better neighborhood; we get out of school; we get married; we have a baby; we have grandchildren; we get divorced; we retire . . .

Then we are frustrated when the job is boring, or the kids aren't mature, or we didn't get the latest promotion.

We tell ourselves that life would be perfect if we had a nicer spouse, car, children, vacation, or retirement package. The truth is: There's no better time to be happy than right now, right here.

This moment is a gift . . . that's why it's called the present.

I like what George Allen, the legendary coach of the Washington Redskins, said. "One of the most difficult things to learn is that life is tough and that life is not fair. No matter who you are or what you do, we're hit with this fact every day. Life . . . every day of your life is full of obstacles, challenges, disappointments, frustrations, and tragedies. Either we take them on and turn them into something good, or they take us down."

Happiness is a moment-by-moment journey, not a destination. Alfred Sloan, legendary leader at General Motors, said it this way: "For a long time it had seemed to me that life was about to begin, but there's always some

(Continued)

Doc's Medicine for Life *(Continued)*

obstacle in the way, something to be gotten through first, some unfinished business. Time still to be served, a debt to be paid. Then life would begin. At last it dawned on me: These obstacles and the opportunities they bring *were* my life."

✓ *Work is wonderful therapy.* Many in America have forgotten that truth, because they've stopped working once they got a job. So, if you're lonely, work. If you're depressed, work. If you're anxious, work. If you're lazy, work. Work elevates you with a sense of productivity and usefulness and gives you a sense of significance.

Commenting upon the lives of centenarians around the world, *Time* reporter Alice Parks, said, "They use their bodies as they were designed: for walking, for working, for being fed from the earth's natural bounty."[3]

Plan so much challenging work that there's just no time to die and no regret when you do.

✓ *If you're not following your own goals, you are following someone else's.* Stated differently, those who do not have goals are controlled by those who do. I repeat this principle in my financial planning seminars, pointing out that there are always people after your money. (Lots of dogs are after them bones.) If you don't have goals—written goals—for your money, someone else does. Who's after your money? The supermarket, salesperson, car dealer, TV evangelist, TV jewel hustler, your kids, your friends, the mall, and the list goes on and on.

If you don't have goals for your own money, your own life, your own time, your own body, someone else does.

And if they're not written down, you don't have goals. You have gauzy wishes, dreams, hopes, but you don't have goals. Goals means you map out your life with pen and paper.

✓ *We cannot predict the future, but we do create it by our moment-to-moment actions.* Actions explode with results. One of the wisest things your mama said to you was, "Go! Go! You might meet somebody." Go. Go to work. Go to school. Go to your computer. Go to your office. Go to the track. Go. Move. Act. Do it.

✓ *Two kinds of people: those who blame God for what they don't have and those who thank God for what they do have.* Those who blame God are EHs, externally handicapped. They're always looking to external things to blame for their lack of success: "bad breaks, my parents, school, older brother, society, country, God, the Bible, my spouse, my tough luck, or my church, my rabbi . . . they're all to blame. They're all hurting me, disappointing me, and crippling me."

Contrast those who thank God for what they do have. Thanking God for what you do have is gratitude, and an attitude of gratitude gives altitude.

✓ *You change who you are, what you are, and where you are . . . by changing what goes into your mind.* It's exactly the same principle of filling your body. Fill it with fat, lard, and grease, and you're fat, slow, and dead. Fill it with rich and pure, and you have a rich, pure life. I have on my dashboard PPP, or it's not for me. PPP stands for "pure, positive, and powerful." Fill your mind only with things that fall into one of these three categories.

(Continued)

Doc's Medicine for Life *(Continued)*

✓ *In every adversity, there is the seed of an equal or greater opportunity.* Life is a symphony, and sometimes that symphony screeches out a sour note. You're the conductor. You take that sour note, and you make it the beginning note of a new and beautiful symphony. You take tragedy, disappointment, adversity, and you say, "How does this help me?" You take pain, frustration, and disappointment, and you say, "What good can I bring out of this?"

Easy?

Hardly, but what's your choice? Bitterness, fear, rage, surrender, or success, service, and self-fulfillment?

✓ *Love is a decision to do what's right, whether you feel like it or not.* Contemporary television and films smother us with the notion that love is a feeling. Love is not a feeling. Love is a decision to do what's right, whether you feel like it or not. Love arises from the will, not the emotions. Losers wait until they feel loving, and then they act loving. Backwards. Winners act loving, and then they feel loving.

✓ *Self-pity is a luxury that winners can't afford.* The longer we stay down, drowning in the ocean of self-pity, the longer it will be before we rise to grab air and rescue others. The reason winners do not luxuriate in self-pity is because we know that other people need us.

✓ *We cannot control other's actions, but we do control our reactions.* Boxers learn this principle early. Hit hard, the amateur boxer feels his ears ringing and brain rattled. He's mad and wants to react swiftly and randomly. If he goes after his opponent swinging wildly, he'll be decked. He must learn to control his reactions. He must learn to go to his corner, dance around, and clear his head before he comes after his opponent.

✓ *What you've got and where you are is plenty good enough to build again.* You don't wait until you have all the resources. You don't wait until you have the perfect opportunity. What you've got and where you are is plenty good enough to build again. It's built upon the principle that "inch by inch, anything's a cinch." Men and women who achieved high levels of success in their service: Moses, Abraham Lincoln, George Washington, Thomas Jefferson, Benjamin Franklin, Thomas Edison, Mother Teresa, Madame Curie, and Mahatma Gandhi dramatized this principle throughout their lives. "Inch by inch, anything's a cinch."

✓ *Goals fire up the imagination and give you the energy to go on.* Goals rise from desire, and desire is fire. I run. When I round that last corner, my legs are cement, my lungs are burning, and salty sweat boils over my lips. I gotta give up. I can't go any farther. Wait. Wait. Wait. There's the finish line. There's the goal. I can see the goal. I can finish.

You made it to your junior year. You can see the goal of the diploma or degree. You've made it 23 years on the job. You can see the retirement date ahead. You've made it to the dissertation stage. You can see the goal of the Ph.D. or M.D. You've made it to the eye-to-eye appointment with the CEO. You can see your marketing plan accepted and your new product financed.

✓ *Two kinds of people: those who believe they can't and those who believe they can—and they're both right.* I catch myself, fellow workers, and family members when we flippantly use the word "can't." There's no such thing as "I

(Continued)

> ## Doc's Medicine for Life *(Continued)*
>
> can't," because "I can't" means "I am helpless." When translated, "I can't" really means, "I will not," or "I don't know how."
>
> If you don't know how, I'll teach you. I'll be glad to help you. If you will not, then we've got a problem with attitude. In that case, we need to review the principles of Doc's Medicine for Life.
>
> ✓ *Tomorrow will be better.* Tomorrow will be better, because faith in the future delivers power in the present.
> ✓ *Most important of all, Work like you don't need the money, love like you've never been hurt, and dance like no one's watching.*

Doc's Medicine for Life touches on the six dynamic needs of every human being. Every human being has three basic needs: air, water, and food in that order, and then he or she has six dynamic needs: (1) the need for security; (2) the need for variety; (3) the need for significance; (4) the need for connectedness; (5) the need to grow; and (6) the need to give.

Now on to the intellectual aspects of aging!

Intellectual

Some folks still think good brains do not equal good bodies and vice versa. Not so! Listen to Socrates, the wise man of Greece and mentor to Plato. This wandering Greek philosopher, who taught Plato and other great thinkers in the late fifth century B.C., was physically powerful and robust.

He served tough stints as a foot soldier in the Athenian infantry and spent much of his later life walking around Greek towns and the countryside, as he advocated his philosophical positions. According to Plato, he typically wore only one single, simple garment, regardless of the season, and usually went barefoot, even in the dead of winter.

Socrates believed in the importance of striking a balance between training the body and the mind, as the following interchange between him and a student, Glaucon, shows:

Socrates: Have you noticed how a lifelong devotion to physical exercise, to the exclusion of anything else, produces a certain type of mind? Just as a neglect of it produces another type? One type tends to be tough and uncivilized, the other soft and oversensitive, and . . .

Glaucon: Yes, I have noticed that excessive emphasis on athletics produces a pretty uncivilized type, while a purely literary and academic training leaves a man with less backbone than is decent.

Socrates: It is the energy and initiative in their nature that may make them uncivilized. If you treat the body properly, it will make you brave. But if you overstrain the body, it will turn young men into tough and uncouth savages, as you would expect.

Glaucon: I agree.

Socrates: The philosophic temperament, on the other hand, is gentle; too much relaxation may produce excessive softness, but if the mind is treated properly the result will be civilized and humane and balanced.

Building Brain Power

- *Learn and grow every day.* Your mind is a muscle: Use it or lose it. Without exercise, your mind rots and dies.

- *Pick up a book, tape, or video.* Here are a few topics to get you started: introduction to calculus; how to build a yo-yo; increase your vocabulary in 30 days; Mediterranean cooking; conversational Japanese; or how to read the entire Bible in one year.

  Also, there's a wonderful company called The Teaching Company (800-TEACH12; http://www.teach12.com). Here's a small sampling of the courses they have: Great Authors of the Western Literary Tradition; Great Artists of the Italian Renaissance; The History of the English Language; and the *Iliad* of Homer.

Seniors Who Keep Brains Alert and Alive

Lillian Prather, 82

Through the people she's known, the places she's been, and the projects she's undertaken, 82-year-old Lillian Prather—former actress and longtime educator—recounts a lifetime of surprises.

While a fine arts student at the University of Texas at Austin, Prather was selected twice as one of the Ten Most Beautiful Girls of the University, in 1942 and 1943. Hollywood actor Walter Pidgeon, fresh from his Oscar-nominated performance in *Mrs. Miniver*, selected the winners in 1943.

Nearly 60 years later, Lillian is still a beautiful girl lending her rich and beautiful voice to the Radio Reading Service of North Texas (North Texas Radio for the Blind). NTRB broadcasts continuous programming for print-impaired listeners and features entertainment and information content that isn't readily available on public radio. Lillian volunteers full time. "It's really good for my brain," she says.

Madonna Wagner, 82

At 82 years of age, Madonna Wagner still has an adventurous spirit. She's proof positive that it's never too late to accomplish a new feat. On December 17, 2002—which happened to coincide with the ninety-ninth anniversary of Orville and Wilbur Wright's first flight—Wagner completed a solo flight. She called each of her children to surprise them with the news of her accomplishment. Only her youngest son knew of her flying lessons, but she had sworn him to secrecy.

Madonna's quest originated during World War II when her husband Tom's flat feet kept him out of the Air Force. He decided to join the local Civil Air Patrol (CAP) to do some flying and show the young boys how to do aircraft mechanics. Madonna followed suit and joined the CAP, earning a staff sergeant's rating, even though raising children preempted flying lessons.

Tom Wagner died four years ago, and her four children—three of them Marine lieutenant colonels—are spread across the country and the world. That leaves Madonna alone but totally in charge of her world and her future.

Wagner has a do-it list, to keep track of daily, weekly, and yearly goals. She doesn't call it a to-do because her motto is simply to "get it done." A current do-it is taking computer classes to help with her writing projects. She checked off another goal when she and a friend set sail on a windjammer cruise in February.

Busy and focused, Madonna is always in motion, claims she's never bored with her own company, and lives every day to its fullest. When asked how she gets it all done, she says firmly, "Don't just talk about it: Do it!"

Philip Johnston

Philip Johnston, esteemed architect, was still designing nouveau structures well into his sixties. And, well into his nineties, this laureate of contemporary American architects continued to create daring urban landscapes and audacious designs. Johnston repeatedly said, "Make no mistake. Age doesn't affect one's artistic or intellectual ability. Really, why would I stop creating and designing when I'm having so much fun?"

- *Take a class* on clogging, square dancing, chess, computer skills, Internet research, building a log house . . . you get the point.

  Tony Robbins pointed out in his tape series *Power Talk* that when you act young and think young, you trick your body into thinking *you are young*. You could be 82 years old and have a brain that is chronologically 52 or 32. You could be 82 years old with good exercise and eating habits, and you could trick your heart into thinking that it's 52 or 32.

Last, but certainly not least, let's focus on strategies to succeed in the spiritual aspects of aging.

Spiritual

The Society of Certified Senior Advisors (CSA) published a compilation of several historic studies on "the importance of God in the lives of seniors." The CSA bulletin said that several Gallup polls, in combination with other studies, concluded:

- Ninety-five percent of seniors say that God is either fairly important or very important in their lives.
- Worship services and Bible studies are attended more by senior citizens than any other age group.
- Spiritual activity, praise, worship, Bible study, and Bible teaching are associated with better health and increased longevity. People in the various studies who did not attend

worship services were four times more likely to die from respiratory diseases, diabetes, or infectious diseases than those who attended.

- Half the volunteer work done for churches, synagogues, or other religious organizations is done by seniors.
- After consideration of all key health and social factors, it was documented that the chances of living longer and better expanded by 28 percent for seniors who attended religious meetings each week.

The *Journal of Gerontology* stated: "Worship attendees were physically healthier, had more support, and lived healthier lifestyles than less frequent attendees. Women had a 35 percent lower risk of death, compared to a 17 percent lower risk for men."

Studies show that people who have a spiritual practice or subscribe to a religious denomination tend to live longer, recover faster from illness, and experience less distress in the face of calamity. This fact has been used for purposes ranging from praising God, to proselytizing, to manipulating and blaming people who are ill. In a recent well-researched and thoughtful book, *God, Faith, and Health: Exploring the Spirituality-Healing Connection* (John Wiley & Sons, 2002), epidemiologist Jeff Levin, Ph.D., said the connection between spirituality, better health, longer living, and happiness is well documented:

- *Healthy lifestyle and social support.* There is evidence that religious people may live longer because they are better stewards of their bodies.
- *Spiritual practice.* Practices such as prayer and meditation have been shown to improve health by promoting physiologic relaxation and strengthening the immune system.

- *Personality.* Most religions teach forgiveness, compassion, and a peaceful composure, which directly benefit health.
- *Cognitive style.* Religions teach faith, hope, and optimism, all of which are associated with better medical outcomes.
- *Supernatural force or intervention.* A spiritual perspective acknowledges the reality that there is a force that is neither physical, emotional, nor mental, and this force is both the source of our aliveness and hope and a Person of power and goodness.

Praying not only has a divine connection to this source, but it has therapeutic consequences as well. It is the oldest of the mind-body techniques. Prayer, by itself, promotes self-esteem, optimism, a sense of control, and a sense of hope. Faith in the future does deliver power and peace in the present. Prayer dramatizes this faith in the future, thus leading to relaxation, self-acceptance, self-nurturing, and spiritual peace. Prayer, in short, is based on *facts,* those rock-hard facts related to our mental health and human progress.

When you practice the strategies listed in all four key aspects (physical, emotional, intellectual, and spiritual), you'll have a good shot at enjoying a healthy 98, staying at home, with good care, slipping off into your final sleep, in your own bed, with loved ones around you.

(Bonus: Studies show that couples who stay physically, emotionally, intellectually, and spiritually active also enjoy the potential and the power to be sexually active—indefinitely.)

Follow these preventative strategies, physical, emotional, spiritual, and intellectual, and you have a good shot at conquering the three Cs: cancer, cardiovascular disease, and crazy. Healthy cells from healthy foods resist cancer. Clean, open, elastic arteries promote healthy hearts, and rich, engaging minds fight dementia.

Euthanasia: The Ultimate Prevention?

Premise: The patient is vegetative and has been declared by two physicians to be incorrigibly terminal. Given this premise, there are four facts that need to be explained:

> *Fact 1:* There is no moral or legal obligation to accept life support.
>
> *Fact 2:* There is no moral or legal command to give life support.*
>
> *Fact 3:* There is no moral or legal obligation prohibiting the removal of life support.*

Again, facts one, two, and three arise from the premise that "the patient is vegetative and has been declared by two physicians to be incorrigibly terminal." There is another fact that has nothing to do with the aforementioned premises.

> *Fact 4:* There is no moral or legal justification for actively killing a person whether that person is in pain or pain-free. Fact 4 relates to the varieties of self-killing called euthanasia, assisted suicide, and sometimes direct suicide.

The euphemism for these is "mercy killing." The true name is "self-killing." Of course, if you take needle, gun, or poison in hand, and without encouragement or assistance from anyone, terminate your life, that's direct suicide. With assistance or encouragement, it's called assisted suicide or euthanasia.

I realize it can be shallow, cavalier, and insensitive to make recommendations on someone else's pain.

---

*Assuming the patient has already stated, in writing, his or her refusal to accept life support.

I know what it's like to be in pain. In a village in Northwest Thailand while I was serving as a Peace Corps medic and teacher in leper colonies, I was attacked with bacillary dysentery for three days. As the cliché says, "I would have had to get better to die." For three days, I was trembling with 104° fever. smashing headaches, nonstop diarrhea, and the inability to hold food and liquids. And I was by myself. I was tempted to end it all.

Then, many years later (back in the States), I was the victim of a whiplash accident. The pain that followed the surgery and the months of rehabilitation eclipsed any pain from the accident itself. I would get up at night and walk the floor begging God to relieve the pain, looking at that aspirin bottle and being tempted to take 40 tablets to end it all rather than the recommended four to mask the pain.

I know what it's like to feel pain. I also know what it's like to have suicide hit close to home.

My mother committed suicide. It was totally unpredictable . . . violent and devastating. She hanged herself. None of us had a clue. I do not judge her.

To the contrary, in my studies of suicide (which I have shared in my ethics classes) I have reached the conclusion that *no sane person commits suicide.* Repeat: No sane person commits suicide. You've got to snap before you make the irreversible decision to end your own life.

That's how powerful the *élan vital* is in us.

On this general subject of self-killing, I disagree with my permissive colleagues in the press and university for several reasons. First, self-killing is not an option because self-killing is cowardice, surrender, and defeat. It demeans one's self, and it demeans the human race. For this reason, every civilized culture has eschewed self-killing as a practice.

Self-killing denies solutions. Tony Robbins tells the story of a doctor who takes on patients declared to be in irreversible pain. He has turned around 400 of them.

Self-killing invokes the excuse: "There is no other way. We had to do it." This is no different from the justification of the rapist who says, "It just got the best of me." Or the thief who says, "I had to. I had to get the money to buy food." As we pointed out earlier, there is always a solution. There is always a solution that is positive and progressive no matter how difficult it may be to find it.

See again the first principle in "Doc's Medicine for Life": Unexpected help comes from unpredictable sources to the person who remains positive, enthusiastic, and cheerful.

Self-killing leaves the survivors with shame and guilt. People who commit self-killing dump a legacy of shame, confusion, and guilt. Typically, the survivors say, "What did *we* do wrong? How could *we* have helped Mom or Dad or Juan or Adele? How could we have prevented it?" I remember counseling with a woman whose son had committed suicide. She had sequestered herself in her room for 18 months.

The only person who knew that her son had committed suicide was the coroner. She made up stories. She wouldn't tell anyone the truth. She was hurt, guilty, confused, and ashamed. She locked herself in her room for 18 months and lost 42 pounds. Mercifully, she heard me on the radio talking about Doc's Medicine for Life. She came in for an appointment, and the first thing I told her was about my own experience with suicide. She opened up and talked, and talked, and talked.

Bottom line: The first step of therapy was to go to the cemetery with her, kneel at the grave, and just let all the guilt go and allow the forgiveness to rush in. You can't just talk healing and forgiveness. Therapy requires action. One of the aftershocks of this lethal legacy is that the survivors begin to hate the person who committed suicide or those who assisted. "Why did you do this? Why did you leave me with all these problems? Why did you leave me with all this guilt?"

Suicide and euthanasia are ostensibly forms of mercy killing. But that's an oxymoron. They are not "merciful" to the perpetrators, the survivors, or the human race.

CHAPTER SUMMARY

There is more to longevity and happiness than just having a lot of money. You must also be mindful of the remaining four aspects of aging and happiness: physical, emotional, intellectual, and spiritual. By combining these elements with financial health, you can live well into your golden years.

So stay active—physically and mentally; build a positive self-image, and enrich your spirit. These are the keys to making it to 98 (or beyond), and living and loving every minute!

ACTION STEPS

- ❑ If you've never exercised a day in your life—or if it's been a while—be sure to consult with your physician to find ways to incorporate exercise into your life.
- ❑ Make a list of all the things you've always wanted to do and cross them off as you complete each one. It's never too late to start!
- ❑ Keep a daily journal. It will keep your mind vibrant, and will serve as a keepsake for your loved ones for years to come.
- ❑ Be daring and take up a new hobby; remember, the only things we regret in life are risks not taken.

❑ Acknowledge that human life is valuable and precious from womb until grave. If you deny this, then nothing in this book makes sense.

CONCLUSION

Now that you know what steps you need to take to ensure that you thrive in all of the five key areas I mentioned, just do it! The strategies work only if you do!

CHAPTER 4

The Plan:
Powerful Strategies That
Protect Profits and
Provide Peace of Mind

The best time to protect your life savings is when you're healthy.
—Harley Gordon, founding member,
National Academy of Elder Law Attorneys

"THERE'S A SUBSTANTIAL CHANCE THAT YOU *CAN* OUTSPEND YOUR wealth," says Dr. Tom Peris, director of the New England Centenarian Study at the Boston Medical Center. And Dr. Peris continues:

Financial health is as much a part of pushing the age barrier as physical health. If you are going to go through all the effort to gain those years, make sure you build a portfolio that's compatible with that. And yet, that may be easier said than done. A recent study by John B. Shovan, the Charles R. Schwab Professor of Economics at Stanford University, reveals that Americans should live longer than current Social Security projections, portending a funding gap for retirees.

You can't care for yourself or a loved one if you're broke—period.

It is important for you to know that you are at risk of six savage attacks on your money. Any one of these attacks can rip you apart (some are inevitable): (1) public disclosure of your finances and personal business; (2) taxes at all levels, including income taxes and estate taxes; (3) lawsuits; (4) government seizure; (5) market risk; (6) inflation and the escalating cost of living.

Table 4.1 is an overview of selected documents and strategies that help shield you from these attacks.

Table 4.1
Bullet Proof Documents

Protective Document/Strategy	Value and Implementation
Living Trust	Protects against public disclosure, family miscommunication, mistakes, and greed. May be used to protect against excessive *estate taxes*. Free from probate.
The Offshore Corporation	Protects against public disclosure, government seizure, and lawsuits.
The Ideal Investment	Protects against market risk, current taxes, and (in some cases) lawsuits. "When the market's up, you're up; when the market's down—you're still up." Possible protection against inflation and cost of living.
The Immediate Annuity	Protects against loss of income. Provides for guaranteed lifetime income. Protects against probate. May be used selectively to protect against Medicaid seizure.

What Is a Living Trust?

Earlier, you agreed with the following:

> I want to control my person and property while I am alive and well. I want to provide for myself and my loved ones *at all times* and, in my final days, give what I own to whom I want, the way I want, and when I want, and save every last tax dollar, attorney fee, and court cost possible. If health-care decisions are made for me by another, I want to appoint—*ahead of time*—the person who makes those decisions and give him or her clear directions on my healthcare choices.

In order to enjoy that control and peace of mind, you may need a living trust, with its ancillary documents properly notarized, funded, and executed. Simply put, a trust is your love letter.

Let's look at a hypothetical example. You are Abe and Sarah Howard, and you are sitting around the kitchen table writing a letter to your kids:

> Dear Mary and Joseph,
>
> Because we love you and love each other, we want to tell you what we want to happen to our money and property in case something happens to us. We are going to die one of these days, you know. And since we're not invincible, one of us could get sick or hurt. Let's take the easy area first. In case both of us die, at the same time, here's what we want to happen.
>
> Sell the house. It's worth about $215,000 and it's paid for. Put the money in the checking account—the one that's in the name of Abe and Sarah Howard Trust. We put you guys

on as secondary trustees. Leave this money in the account until all the money comes in from all the places we're going to talk about in this letter.

Mary, you can have Sarah's car, and Joe, you can have Abe's car. Mary, you can have the computer, cookbooks, tennis rackets, the green photo album, the pictures in the den, and all our cassettes, CDs, videos, and stuff like that. Joe, you can have the golf clubs, all the tools, Abe's desk, all the pictures in Abe's study, the burgundy photo album, and the old pickup (Good luck!). These are all the things each of you have asked for over the years.

The rest of the stuff—here's what you should do: Flip a coin. We're serious. Call it "heads." If Mary gets "heads," she'll go first and pick one item in the house; then Joe will pick one item, then Mary, then Joe, back and forth until you have divided up all our belongings. If there's nothing either of you want, give them to the church.

Cash in all the IRAs, annuities, and CDs. We left written permission with the banks and annuity companies. You're listed as the co-beneficiaries. Take all the money and put it into the checking account. It should be about $263,000 for the IRAs, $116,000 in a joint annuity, and a $71,000 CD.

Total for the house and all the rest of it should be $565,000! Split it in half between the two of you, about $282,000 each.

Mary, with your $282,000, give $28,000 to the church and tell them to use it for foreign relief efforts. Set aside $15,000 for Mickey's college education and $22,500 for Erica's. (Mickey shouldn't need as much because he's got more time to let it grow.) Tell Mickey and Erica that this money is to be used for college or, if they prefer, a technical school. If they don't go to college or technical school, they can use it to start a business.

They cannot use it for any other purpose. If they don't go to college or technical school and they don't want to start the new business, they give the money back to you, Mary. And Mary, after you take out $28,000 for the church, $22,500 for Erica, $15,000 for Mickey, that should leave $216,500—which you can do with as you want.

Joe, with your $282,000, take $28,000 and give it to the Salvation Army. Take $75,000 and put in a special needs trust for Toby. Take $16,500 and put it in a college education fund for Sean—with the same regulations we gave Mary to use for college education/technical school/or to start a business. That'll leave you with about $162,500, which you can do with as you want.

We know it's not necessary to say this, but if anyone fusses or argues about any of this, no one gets anything! Of course, if one of us predeceases the other, then the remaining spouse gets full control of all assets and property.

In case both of us become disabled, we instruct Mary to get money from whatever part of our accounts or belongings she wants in order to take care of any extra medical expenses we might have. In other words, she has the financial power of attorney. If one of us gets to the point where someone has to "pull the plug," we also give Mary the medical power of attorney.

If we're both out of it (or if there's only one of us left and dying), or Mary's not around, we give Joe the medical power of attorney (i.e., the right to tell the doctors when to terminate any life support system).

You know what Abe and Sarah just did? They wrote their revocable living trust. Some folks call it their "family trust" or "living trust," or just plain "trust."

Abe and Sarah wrote down what they wanted to do with their

property and money. (If they had minor children, they would have also written down the name or names of the guardians.) These instructions kick in whether Abe and Sarah are *dead* or *alive*. Of course, the trust Abe and Sarah wrote at their kitchen table is not full and final. There's a lot (a lot!) more needed to list all the wishes and assets of Abe and Sarah.

I made Abe and Sarah's "trust" simple—very simple—to demonstrate that a trust is personal and flexible. When you do yours, do it with an attorney skilled in estate law, and he will make sure you identify all the critical areas of your life.

Do not buy the fiction that you can do the trust yourself! (How to Write Your Own Living Trust for only $59.95! Yeah, right.) Get a lawyer!

To see the value of a living trust, here's a side-by-side comparison with a will in Table 4.2.

"I Want to Get a Trust, but . . ."

Objection #1 "Trusts benefit only rich folk." Not so. Unless you're living on welfare, literally anyone can enjoy the benefits of a trust. Because the main benefit of a trust has nothing to do with money or property. The benefits of a trust are: privacy, control, flexibility, special needs, simplicity, peace of mind, and estate protection.

Objection #2 "Probate is simple and cheap in _____ (You name the state.). A simple will's all you need." Wrong again. Again, the issue's not cheap versus expensive! Most importantly, the owners of a trust *have* privacy, control, and flexibility. The owners of a will do not. Law professor Charles A. Saunders said it right: "Contrary to popular misconceptions, trusts do not have to be expensive to maintain, nor do they have to be inflexible."

Probating the will may not be simple after all. All it takes is one

Table 4.2
Trusts versus Wills

Living Trust	Will
Private. Abe and Sarah have the original. That's it. No one—not their lawyer, kids—no one has a copy, unless Abe and Sarah choose to give them a copy. Abe and Sarah are the *trustmakers* (or trustors). Those are the people who have the money and property. They are also the *trustees*, the people authorized to carry out the instructions of the trustmakers. (Here, the *trustmakers* and *trustees* are the same.) They appoint successor trustees to carry out their instructions and they appoint beneficiaries, that is, the people who benefit from the trust.	*Public.* When you die, your will is on display at the county clerk's office. This is because w-a-a-y back, 800 years ago in English law, wills were invented for the protection of creditors. Creditors want to look at what you've got, so they can grab it to pay what you owe. Wills were not invented for the benefit of the owner, but for the benefit of the creditor. And you don't have to be a creditor. *Anyone* can look at your will. This explains why widows will have folks calling. Somebody's been reading Dear Departed Jeb's will and knows he's got cash or property. So, they call, pretending to be some creditor, and say, "Oh, he didn't tell you about his $8,100 pledge to help ABC or his contract to buy XYZ?" The grieving widow falls for it.
No probate. (Probate's the expensive, irritating process of taking the departed person's will to court.) It usually involves an attorney or two, a CPA to calculate the value of the assets, a judge, and an executor.	*Guaranteed probate.* I have got to explain this, because once a day, I'll have a client call me to say, "We don't need to worry about probate. We have a will." No! No! No! A will *guarantees* probate.
Flexible. When you and your spouse want to change your trust, you sit around the kitchen table and write your changes. Get it notarized, witnessed, and approved by your estate planning attorney. Normally, if you are using the same attorney, it should be quite easy and not involve any additional expense.	*Inflexible.* Want changes? Drive down to Mr. Lawyer's big office building and have a "codicil" drawn—takes time—takes money.

Table 4.2 *(Continued)*

Living Trust	Will
Good at death or disability. In the event you become disabled, the living trust takes effect. It designates a medical power of attorney in your trust, who will be responsible for all of your medical decisions in the event that you're incapable of making your own.	*You've got a will and you're disabled—Tough!* Will's no good. Gotta die before will takes effect. Court will appoint a guardian—whom you may not know or may not like—to care for your affairs while you're disabled. "Doc, I've got that covered. I've got a will and have power of attorney set up." So what? When you die, the power of attorney dies. By the way, ever try to get a bank or brokerage firm to honor a power of attorney? Good luck.
Freedom from estate taxes. Structure it right and you can save your estate hundreds of thousands of dollars when you die. I am not a lawyer or a CPA, but working with lawyers, I have seen how good estate planning can save thousands, or even millions, of dollars. Details in how to do this are beyond the scope of this brief book. A good attorney will show you how.	*Big estate? Simple will?* Super estate taxes! Up to 55%. And Uncle IRS wants his money in nine months, whether the value of your house, land, stock, or mutual funds is up or down. Objection: "A complex will can address this." Answer: Yes, but two probates will be required.
Special needs. Someone in your family with special needs—illness, injury, handicap? Your trust can take care of them whether you're dead or alive.	A will can have a trust added to it, but then again, it won't take effect until probated.
Portable. Good in *all* states.	*State-specific.* Need a new will in every state.

Jerry, your mad and jealous cousin, to show up in court and claim, "Hey, Abe told me he was leaving that $72,000 CD to me, and I've got witnesses to prove it." Jerry may be lyin', lyin', lyin', but if he sounds good, he can tie up the probate process for weeks, months, years.

In the meantime, someone's trying to get the estate settled, to get the rightful beneficiaries their money, and pay the family lawyer. The grieving widow's trying to get money to live on, but Jerry's in the way.

I know because grieving widows end up in my office, crying and pleading with me to help them find a way to get their *rightfully owned* money and *rightfully owned* property out of probate. They need the money to live on, and they don't want to be kicked out of their *rightfully owned* house.

Sure, probate in your state may be simple and cheap, but why take the chance? A living trust can help prevent the disgruntled Jerrys of the world from showin' up and screwin' up the settlement of Daddy and Momma's estate.

To say "In my state, probate's no problem" is like saying, "In my state, surgery's no problem." You enter the hospital for a procedure. Two ways—let's say—they can fix you: surgery or nonsurgery.

"How many of you would prefer the nonsurgery approach?" I ask my seminar students. All hands raised. Why this unanimous preference?

We know that surgery always carries potential dangers: aspirating, blood clots, staph infections, or cardiac arrest. Not to mention the cost, pain, worry, and inconvenience.

Ditto with probate. With probate, you invite danger. *Anyone* can show up at probate and contest your loved one's will. The will is public, its proceeds are tempting, and its settlement is often lengthy, hostile, and totally unpredictable.

Objection #3   "A trust is more expensive." Absolutely. I'm not a lawyer and I don't know what state you live in, but ballpark, a trust normally will run three or four times the cost of a will—unless you do a "do-it-yourself" will or a "do-it-yourself" trust, which is a do-it-yourself nightmare.

Trying to do your own legal planning is like trying to do your own appendectomy. It's too close and too painful. And you don't have the expertise to do it, despite the claims of the $59.95 E-Z Trust Kit, or Do Your Own Will Manual.

A will may be cheaper, but it triggers the expensive probate process.

Some lawyers in some places can charge up to 6 percent of the value of your estate. Your estate (house, cars, savings, IRA) is worth a modest $300,000 (6 percent × $300,000 = $18,000).

Now, throw in your life insurance—yes, your life insurance, a $200,000 death benefit, let's say. Some folks forget that life insurance proceeds (the death benefit) is part of your estate. But it sure is.

Now, let's say this lawyer charges only 3 percent (instead of 6 percent). Three percent of $500,000 (estate of $300,000 + $200,000 life insurance) is $15,000. Last I checked, $15,000 was a chunk of change and much higher than the $2,000 to $2,500 a trust might have cost. And your kids or someone has to come up with the probate fees—*immediately*—to pay for probating the will.

Objection #4   "A trust's no good unless you get it funded." That's right—and a car's no good unless you shove the key in the ignition.

Funding means: Abe and Sarah set up The Abe and Sarah Greenwood Revocable Living Trust, dated 8-22-05. The trust is done right, with an attorney, and it's properly notarized.

Abe and Sarah then take the notarized cover pages to their

bank (the first two to three pages, not the whole thing; remember, the contents of a trust are private).

Their checking account no longer says "Abe & Sarah Greenwood, 123 Desert Way, Paradise, U.S.A." It now reads, "The Abe and Sarah Greenwood Trust, 123 Desert Way, Paradise, U.S.A."

And the Social Security number Abe and Sarah had on the old "Abe and Sarah Greenwood" checking account is the same Social Security number carried on the new checking account.

Their house is probably registered as follows: Owners, Abe and Sarah Greenwood. They take the cover document of the new trust to the courthouse and get the house re-registered as "Owner, The Abe and Sarah Greenwood Trust."

They do this with all their accounts and all their properties. This is called "funding."

If you're not going to follow through to get your trust funded, then get your attorney or financial advisor to do it for you. If you're not going to do this, don't do a trust.

Parties in a Trust

Every trust is comprised of three parties: trustmaker, trustees, and beneficiaries. The *trustmakers* (or *trustors*) are the people who own the money and property. They're the owners of the estate, in this case, Abe and Sarah Greenwood.

The *trustees* are the people en-"trusted" by the trustmakers to carry out their instructions. The trustees manage the estate of the trustmakers.

The trustmakers and the trustees are usually the same. Abe and Sarah *own* the estate of Abe and Sarah and they *manage* the estate of Abe and Sarah. They will appoint successor trustees. These are the people who will manage the estate if Abe and Sarah are dead or disabled.

The successor trustee is the person (or persons) whom Abe and Sarah *trust* to carry out their wishes. Successor trustees are legally bound to carry out the instructions of the trustmakers. No guesswork there.

The third party in the living trust is the *beneficiary* (or *beneficiaries*). These are the people who get the *benefit* of the property and money as instructed by the trustmakers and fulfilled by the trustees. While living, Abe and Sarah are the exclusive beneficiaries of their own trust. Abe and Sarah can designate other beneficiaries, if they desire.

Two Stories

Still don't see the value in creating a trust? Let me share two stories with you.

"Doc, did you see the paper this weekend? I mean, the obituary about Jay?" The voice on the other end was Mrs. Jay (Pam) Kearns, a familiar client.

"No, no, I didn't, Pam."

Pam and Jay Kearns had been clients for 10 years, the last two of which Jay had been in and out of Mayo Clinic with leukemia and multiple complications.

"He died last Thursday, Doc."

"Pam, I'm so sorry to hear that. I am *so sorry* to hear that. No one fought a harder fight for so long as Jay did. How are you doing, and what are the arrangements?"

"Doc, I just didn't have a chance to call you. The funeral was in Oklahoma, where Jay grew up. I really need to find out, though—I'm going to see my CPA this afternoon. What do I need to do to get the money and everything in my name?"

Long pause.

"Pam, you remember those meetings you, me, and Jay had—oh, I think it was three-and-a-half or four years ago. You'd come to one of my programs on safe estate planning, and we talked about trusts?"

"Yes? Yes."

"Well, that paperwork that you and the attorneys—remember when I got Mr. Thorn to help you? The estate planning attorney? And then we took those documents, and you sent it to your bank, your title company, your checking account, your mutual fund account. Remember? That took care of everything, Pam. That took care of everything. You don't have to do a thing. Those checks that you've been receiving say, 'To Jay and Pamela Kearns, Living Trust Account.' You're a trustmaker, you're a trustee. You just continue to put that money in your account and spend it like you always have. Just continue to sign your checks like you always have. You don't change anything on your house, your car, your mutual funds. You're listed as the primary beneficiary on Jay's accounts. *You don't have to do anything.*"

I was 63 miles away, and I could hear her breathe a deep sigh of relief. I could feel the tension melting from her muscles. At a time of tragic loss, the last thing you need is to worry about money.

Marge came to one of my programs too late. She visited my office a few days after the program and said: "My husband died. I found his stock certificates, and here's his will. The stock certificates were in his name. He had a will done a long time ago when we were living in New York."

Fortunately, none of Marge's children or relatives were challenging the will or challenging ownership of any of her accounts. But all she had was a small checking account, a smaller savings account, and a Social Security check. Her challenge, however, was to live on that Social Security check while she got this out-of-state will probated. She then had to get the stock certificates issued in her name, so she could cash them and live on them.

It took nine months—nine months of anxiety and worry while she was still having to deal with the grief of losing her lifetime mate of 43 years.

Marge and her husband Richard did not have a lot of money, and so at some time, someone probably told them, "Don't worry about doing a trust." But a trust is exactly what Marge needed at that critical and painful time in her life.

Won't Financial Powers of Attorney Do the Same Thing?

"My financial planner, or attorney, or CPA says all I need is a simple will and powers of attorney." Maybe you, or your financial planner, or your CPA, or your attorney has not sat where I've sat. We've already talked about the limitations of a will. A power of attorney is limiting, arbitrary, unreliable, and in many cases, unenforceable.

Ninety-two-year-old Tyrone called and asked me to stop by his house on my way home. I stopped by, and he gave me his mutual fund statement, asking me to transfer his $42,156.12 from his mutual fund investment to his local bank. I attempted to do so, and Tyrone and I discovered that the $42,156.12 was gone.

It seems that he earlier had given his 46-year-old granddaughter power of attorney, presumably to take care of him. Apparently Granddaughter had met a hotshot who wanted a hot rod car and hustled Granddaughter to buy it—with her grandfather's money. Powers of attorney produce some surprises at the very time you don't need surprises.

When You Give Someone Power of Attorney, You Give Them a Blank Check!

Children of clients come to me with a power of attorney asking me to send their power of attorney to Big Bank, or Big Broker, or

Big Insurance Company to get money out to care for Mom and Dad. (It's legitimate. Checks are to be made to the nursing home, or clinic, or hospital, caring for Mom and Dad.) So I send the power of attorney to the Big Broker, or Big Bank, or Big Insurance Company.

They call: "Dr. Gallagher, sorry we can't help your client, because these powers of attorney are over 90 days old." (Or they use some other delaying tactic.)

The fiduciaries who receive these powers of attorney have great latitude and great power in blocking the enforcement of powers of attorney. They don't want the money to leave Big Broker, or Big Bank, or Big Insurance Company!

You might say, "Let 'em try it on me, and I'll sue 'em!"

Good for you! And six months or a year later when you finally get to court, the damage has already been done. You weren't able to get to the money you needed to take care of your loved one.

This probably wouldn't have happened if Mom and Dad had owned a trust: properly completed, notarized, funded, and executed. A properly worded trust can help protect your money and property from family members who misunderstand your wishes or misuse your money. Done right, a trust can also help offset estate taxes and probate. A properly executed trust can have plurality of secondary trustees (kind of like a check-and-balance), all of whom can help honor your wishes.

Offshore Corporations: The Ultimate Asset Protection?

As noted, a trust can protect your money and property from family members who may misunderstand your wishes or misuse your money. It can also help with the avoidance of probate. A worse threat, however, to your money and property may come from lawsuits and seizures. The average American will be sued five times in his lifetime.

There are more lawsuits filed in the United States than in all other countries combined. And if a suit against you prevails, you end up on welfare (Medicaid) or dependent on your family or both.

"But I'm innocent!"

Doesn't matter.

When you are the target of a lawsuit (i.e., when you are the defendant), your defense will be $10,000, $50,000, $100,000, $250,000, or more. That can wipe out many families and plunge them into poverty and depression.

You can protect yourself from being the target of money-hungry lawyers and insatiable tax collectors, or crusading regulators.

Ryan Whitehurst worked hard at his profession and accumulated the rewards that go with success. Then a jealous and disgruntled neighbor named him as a defendant in a lawsuit and threatened to "take him for everything he owned." But after Ryan had a talk with the plaintiff's attorney, the suit was quietly dropped. The reason? In spite of his apparent wealth, he doesn't legally "own" anything that a lawsuit or court judgment can take. Ryan had the foresight to shelter his assets in a judgment-proof *international business corporation*—an IBC.

Why take a chance on losing everything you own? Under the U.S. legal system, the deck is stacked in favor of the plaintiff and against the defendant (that's you). That's why so many lawyers specialize in contingency fee lawsuits in which they are paid a percentage of whatever they win for their clients. This encourages the filing of spurious lawsuits. Since a new lawsuit is filed every 30 seconds, the average business owner or professional person stands a chance of being sued several times in his or her lifetime. Under the current system, any suit, no matter how apparently worthless, can result in a ruinous judgment. Remember the woman who was awarded $2.5 million after *she* spilled hot coffee on *herself*?

Once a lawsuit has been filed, the law will not allow you to move your assets. You must act ahead of time to protect what you own before it comes under attack. The best way to protect your assets is not to *own* any. Only if you own an asset is it vulnerable to attack. If you don't *own* it, but merely *control* it, then the asset is well protected.

Some individuals try to accomplish this by forming a corporation. But most trial lawyers will tell you that, except in Nevada, a U.S. corporation offers little or no privacy or liability protection. U.S. corporate documents are public record and any good investigator or search firm can easily find the bank accounts, investments, real estate, and other assets held by the corporation. The U.S. corporate veil is routinely ignored by the courts, and lawsuits are generally filed against the corporation and any of its officers. *If the plaintiff prevails, you would lose everything.*

True story: Jacquelyn Parker found herself under attack by several collection agencies who had succeeded in getting judgments against her and her partners. Her stateside corporation successfully protected her assets from the collection lawyers. But when the IRS decided money was owed them, they convinced a federal judge to pierce Jacquelyn's corporate veil and hold the officers of her stateside corporation personally liable for some of the alleged taxes due. And Jacquelyn could do nothing.

Note: That U.S. federal judge who authorized the IRS seizure would have had no power to seize the assets of an IBC in the Bahamas!

Judgment-proof your assets to avoid ruinous lawsuits. The first step in becoming judgment-proof is to get your assets out of your personal ownership. One of the best ways to do this is to transfer your money, investments, vehicles, property, and other assets into an offshore corporation. This is a legal entity that you control.

Lawyers for plaintiffs will continue to pursue only cases they believe will pay off, not those against judgment-proof defendants. The best way of getting the plaintiff's lawyer to accept a token settlement is to convince the lawyer that your assets are truly beyond the lawyer's reach.

By forming an offshore international business company based in the Bahamas (for example), you create a legal entity to hold assets and even do business. And no one knows who the beneficial owner is. All of the investigative agencies, which help trial lawyers, ex-spouses, ex-business partners, and creditors locate the wealth of the defendants they want to sue, will not be able to find your sheltered accounts and assets. This makes you a poor prospect for a lawsuit or seizure.

Judgments of U.S. courts are not recognized in the Bahamas. Even if the judgment of a U.S. lawsuit should somehow target your IBC, offshore courts (i.e., Bahamas, Cayman Islands) do not recognize U.S. court judgments.

Under this protection, you can cut the cost of liability insurance. This ability to protect your assets is the reason many doctors, professional businesspeople, and owners of small businesses have discovered IBCs as an effective way to lower liability insurance coverage. This can save them tens of thousands of dollars in premiums each year.

Who should use an offshore corporation? People who work hard for their financial rewards and who want to keep their assets secret and out of reach of lawyers and lawsuits or seizure by government agencies, as well as:

- Anyone who is the potential target of a lawsuit.
- Anyone anticipating a costly divorce.
- Anyone with a high net worth.
- Anyone paying high premiums for liability insurance.
- Professionals and business owners.

- Individuals who need to keep their financial affairs private.
- Professionals working abroad.
- Companies selling products abroad.
- Anyone needing to separate high-risk investments from other assets.
- Anyone wishing to buy securities or precious metals not available to U.S. citizens.
- Artists, inventors, and holders of copyrights, patents, or trademarks.

"Stop right there, Doc! You've giving advice that is illegal, unethical, and dangerous. You're telling people how to hide money and evade taxes. You're also making people afraid of government regulators unnecessarily."

Read my lips: I'm not giving legal advice. I'm reminding you of information that's already in the public domain. I can't say if this information is suitable for you. I can remind you of this: It is very ethical to protect your money, so you can protect yourself and your loved ones. I like the practical and comprehensive reminder of the New Testament quote that says, "Love your neighbor."

Is that what it says? No, it says, "Love your neighbor . . . as yourself." We have a biblical, healthy, and intensely practical responsibility to take care of ourselves.

And what about those government regulators? We acknowledge that we need certain government agencies and certain government regulators for limited and beneficial purposes (like highway safety). The problem with government regulators is encapsulated in Lord Acton's phrase, "Power tends to corrupt; absolute power corrupts absolutely."

Many government regulators unfortunately take the position, "You're guilty until you prove yourself innocent," so they seize money, property, vehicles, businesses, personal records, and so on, and then challenge you to take them to court! Sure, you can go to court and prove your innocence.

So then it's *John Q. Citizen* or *Jane Q. Citizen vs. United States.* Unless you're Microsoft, you don't have the time, money, or legal guns to take on the United States of America, which really means taking on a crusading government regulator who resents your success. And sometimes it's not a federal regulator. It could be city, county, or state.

The truth is, it is routine for some government regulators to seize first, then ask questions later. Don't let it happen to you. You will have lost the revenue and the records to be able to defend yourself if everything is seized upfront.

Keep the following in mind: An IBC has nothing to do with tax evasion. Tax evasion is illegal. Don't do it. An IBC has nothing to do with hiding contraband from government regulators. Don't traffic in contraband. But do protect your power and your privacy.

An IBC has nothing to do with tax avoidance. You don't need an IBC to utilize those legal and popular strategies of tax avoidance already available, namely: tax-free, tax-credit, tax-neutral, or tax-deferred investments.

In sum, an IBC provides *lawsuit* protection and *privacy* protection.

Grow Old, but Not Poor: Your Financial Health

"Doc, I can't start all over again."

"Doc, I'm going to have to buy a car in a few years."

"Doc, we've got to get this house paid off, and we want to help our kids and our grandkids some, but we don't want to risk any money."

"Doc, our prescriptions are running about $500 a month. Where are we going to get the money to pay for that? Social Security will never cover it."

"Doc, where are we going to get the money to take care of Mom and Dad?" Or husband and wife. "We lost so much money in mutual funds and variable annuities, where are we going to get the money?"

These are the typical comments I hear from my clients and callers to my radio show. Indeed, how *can* you build wealth that will potentially produce above-average returns *and* protect your principal?

How do you do that? Let's assume that you are either unable or unwilling to take out long-term care insurance. How are you going to *make sure* that you have enough money to pay for the expensive and extended home health care?

You're *not* going to do it through CDs. At a 2- or 3-percent return, you'll never make enough money. You're not going to do it through mutual funds or variable annuities. You're probably not going to go through stocks or bonds, because when a bear market comes—not if, but when—you potentially will lose tons of money as folks did in 1973–1974, 1987–1988, 1994–1995, and 2000–2003. It's too risky. You've got to own the Ideal Investment.

What Your Broker Does Not Want You to Read

The Amazing Financial Power of _____

You fill in the blank. Day trading? Oil? Raw land? Precious metals? Options? Art? Antiques? CDs?

Before I tell you, you tell me. Why would anyone *not* want to own the Ideal Investment? Not perfect because each investment has its own pros and cons, benefits and limitations, advantages and disadvantages, but ideal. What has this amazing financial power?

Before you answer: I sell you a house. It costs $100,000. And I tell you, "Nine years from now, I guarantee, I will buy this house back (if you want to sell) for $118,000, even if:

The windows are busted and paint is peeled.
It's infested with termites and rats.
It's just a slab on dirt.

It doesn't matter. Nine years from now, I'll buy it back for a minimum of $118,000."

It gets better.

Value goes up to, say, $270,000 net. You started with $100,000. It grew to $270,000. That's a gain of $170,000. We nearly tripled your money and with a guarantee that you could never lose your principal! At the end of nine years, you choose: You get the $270,000 or the $118,000. Obviously, real estate values are up. Your $100,000 home is worth $270,000. You take the $270,000. If real estate values are down, your $100,000 home is worth, say, $72,000 (just like all your neighbors'). You don't take $72,000. You take $118,000—that is, if you want to sell. If the market's up, you're up. If the market's down, you are still up! Worst case, you get $118,000. Most likely, based on past performance, you get $270,000.

By the way, while it was growing, you got monthly income if you wanted it. Call it "rent."

This is a win-win, a home purchase with no downside risk. Now substitute "S&P 500[1] equity annuity" for the word "home."

While it's growing, the profits are tax deferred and those profits are reinvested, meaning that they are not added to your Social Security income. The entire investment is protected from lawsuits (in some states). The entire investment is free from probate and free from market risk.

Again, "free from probate" means that the value of the investment (principal plus profit) passes directly to your beneficiary.

No courts.
No lawyers.
No CPAs.
No hassle.

What is it again? It is an equity-index, tax deferred, and growth strategy called the equity index annuity. Or simply the Index Annuity for short. It's been around a long time, and it works similar to the home illustration.

It's your Ideal Investment.

You put in $100,000. The $100,000 is placed in an investment that tracks the S&P 500. (The S&P 500 is a measure of stock market growth. The index takes the top 500 stocks and holds them long-term. You track your $100,000 in the market by way of this equity index annuity.)

Nine years are over. (Or one year, two years, five years, seven years—whatever term you chose.) The stock market crashes. Your friends wail and moan about their stocks, bonds, mutual funds, and 401(k)s. The market is down 30 percent. Their $100,000 is now worth $70,000.

Not you. Your $100,000 is worth $118,000, at least. You get bragging rights for your smart, risk-free way of participating in the market indirectly, while protecting your principal and profits. If the market had rocketed, you would have reaped even bigger profits . . . and protected them.

Fifteen percent of the time, the market is down; 15 percent of the time, the market is flat, and 70 percent of the time, the market is up. The index annuity captures that upside potential, while protecting the principal on the downside. In this example, the upside potential escalated your $100,000 to $270,000.

So, what's the catch?

Good question. You know there's no perfect investment. Each has its benefits and limitations, pros and cons. You examine each investment, including this one. You examine its advantages and disadvantages, benefits and limitations, pros and cons. See Table 4.3.

This ideal investment is based upon Warren Buffett's common sense rules:

Rule #1: *Protect your principal.*
Rule #2: See rule number one.

When you protect the principal, you don't have to recover from an 18 percent, 38 percent, or 68 percent loss! Protecting your principal is a strategy that's similar to the tortoise and hare strategy. Constantly protecting the principal means you are constantly making progress. It may be slow at times, unexciting, but it has shown that it does prevail over risky strategies of stocks and bonds, mutual funds, and variable annuities, particularly for people who want a safety net underneath their money.

What Your Banker Does Not Want You to Read

Think "CD." You put $100,000 in a one-year bank CD. You get a 5.5 percent return at the end of the year. You have your $100,000 plus $5,500 interest.

Table 4.3
Pros and Cons of an Index Annuity

Benefits	Limitations
Participates in growth of stock market while giving a guarantee that you can never lose your principal.	Nine years (or whatever term you chose). Don't put short-term dollars in here. You *can* get out occasional income, but don't even think about ripping out the whole principal for nine years, or you'll be hit with surrender fees. This is an advantage, because it's perfect for money dedicated for retirement or other long-term purposes, subject to annuity rules.
Regardless of losses in stock market (down 10 percent, 50 percent, 75 percent—it doesn't matter), this will guarantee protection of principal *plus* money market rates (approximate) each year. Like Will Rogers said, "I ain't so much concerned about the return *on* my investment as I am about the return *of* my investment."	Not suitable for the Greedy Gambler. The G.G. says, "Heck, when the market goes up, I want it to go way up. I don't want just the gains of the S&P 500 or some portion of it. I want the whole enchilada, heartburn and all."
No current taxes to pay.	Some EIAs have fees, caps, or low participation rates. You want to own an EIA with no fees, no caps, and no limiting participation rates, if possible.
No phantom taxes to pay. Phantom taxes work like this: In the year 2000, many investors saw their mutual funds lose 50 percent of their value. Yet the mutual fund company declared capital gains and dividends for the year 2000. Those capital gains and dividends were reported as profits even though they were down—way down—in value. You have to pay taxes on profits, even though you lost money.	
No probate.	

Table 4.3 *(Continued)*

Benefits	Limitations
No sales charges.	
No management fees.	
No churning. Churning is the stockbroker practice of buying and selling, buying and selling, buying and selling, for purposes of making money for the broker and the broker/dealer—not necessarily for the client. That is the reason the potential of a Guaranteed Index Annuity may be something a broker does not want you to know about. There are no sales charges, no management fees, and no possibility of churning. He or she may find his or her own livelihood threatened.	
Income available.	
Free from lawsuits.	
A "sleep-well-at-night" investment. You never have to worry about bad news belched up from the press.	
At the end of the plan period, a guaranteed income stream can be set up that you cannot outlive. A guaranteed income for you or your spouse—forever. Or you can take out the whole thing.	
The cherry on top of the whipped cream on top of the EIA sundae is this: Some EIAs give a 5 to 10 percent bonus *up front.* You deposit $100,000. Your immediate value is $105,000 to $110,000, depending on the product. You never lose that bonus (or the resulting profits) provided you stay with the EIA for the prescribed period of time.	

You have $105,500. Or do you?

The $5,500 is *total return*—not net return. ("Net return" is what you put into your pocket.)

See, you've got to pay taxes on the $5,500. Let's be conservative. Let's say you're in the 20 percent bracket (20 percent × $5,500 = $1,100).

So, $5,500 (what you thought you earned) − $1,100 = $4,400. On a $100,000 investment, $4,400 is a 4.4 percent return. That won't cut it.

It gets worse. The 4.4 percent is the net rate of return, not the real rate of return. The real rate of return is what "really" ends up in your pocket after taxes *and inflation*. Inflation runs about 4 percent. That means that your money loses 4 percent of its purchasing power every year.

Your net rate of return was $4,400. Subtract another $4,000 (4 percent) lost in inflation and you're left with a real rate of return of $400. That's .04 percent on $100,000.

How can a CD annuity potentially improve on that? Let me count the ways:

Higher rate of return.
No current taxes.
Income you cannot outlive.
No probate.
No addition to adjusted gross income (AGI) by Social Security.
Lawsuit protection.

Higher rate of return. Normally, when you find a bank CD paying 4 percent, you'll find a CD annuity paying 6 percent. Find a bank CD paying 5 percent, and there's a CD annuity paying 7 percent. Find a bank CD paying 2 percent, and you'll find a CD annuity paying 4 or 5 percent—you get the picture.

No current taxes. Just like it says, *no current taxes*. You reinvest the interest and you get *no* 1099. No 1099 = no interest to report to Uncle IRS. See Table 4.4.

Would you rather have $4,400 or $7,700? (And that's just the first year!)

Question: What about inflation and the CD annuity? Won't inflation eat into the $7,700? Yes, so you do what thousands of investors do. Balance your investment! Put $50,000 into the fixed high-interest CD annuity, and put $50,000 into an index annuity for its potential growth—a growth pattern that has exceeded inflation and taxes.

Question: Don't you have to pay taxes sometime? Probably, depending upon how it's structured. But even then, tax deferral has amazing power.

Consider the case just outlined. You made $7,700. If you had to pay current taxes, that's $1,540 you would have had to send to Uncle IRS ($7,700 × 20 percent = $1,540). But you didn't send $1,540; you kept it. You got to make money *off* that $1,540, which compounds every year.

In two years, that's an extra $3,080; in five years, an extra $7,500; in 10 years, an extra $15,400.

No probate. On each annuity, there is a space for you to state the "primary beneficiary" (or beneficiaries) and "secondary

Table 4.4
Side-by-Side Comparison: Bank CD vs. CD Annuity

Bank CD	CD Annuity
$100,000 @ 5.5 percent.	$100,000 @ 7.5 percent.
Equals $5,500.	Equals $7,700.
Less taxes (20 percent bracket = $1,100 in taxes).	$7,700 is reinvested, so *no* taxes.
Means you get $4,400 in your pocket, for net return.	Means you get $7,700 in your pocket, for net return.

beneficiary" (or beneficiaries). Regular bank CDs do not have beneficiary designations.

Look at the difference: You are the owner of a regular $100,000 bank CD; you die. The distribution of this $100,000 CD will require the services of a judge, a CPA, a lawyer, or all three, plus a potentially costly settlement period, with tons of money and time.

With the CD annuity (and its stated beneficiaries), your money goes *directly* to your beneficiary or beneficiaries. There is:

No probate.
No court.
No CPAs.
No lawyers.
No time delay.
No possibility of disgruntled relatives jumping in to claim their prize.

No addition to adjusted gross income (AGI) as part of Social Security income. On your $100,000, you earned $7,500. You reinvest it in your $100,000, now totaling $107,500. It's yours to keep. No reporting is necessary for Social Security purposes.

No lawsuits. How come O.J.'s playing golf on sun-splashed courses in Florida? Where'd he get the money? Remember, he lost the *civil* case! All was taken from him, including his Heisman trophy. They stripped him. But they couldn't seize his annuity.

Years before, O.J. had listened to a financial guy who told him, "Hey, O.J., put some of your money in an annuity. Technically, it's considered an *insurance product,* so it grows tax-deferred, free from probate and *free from litigation.*"

Many investors with large cash flows and potentially large liabilities (like doctors, business professionals, etc.) enjoy the legal creditor-protection of annuities. Some states are better than others. Check with your local attorney.

Flexible Premium Annuities

You deposited a lump sum, one time, in your *index* annuity, the Ideal Investment. You deposited a lump sum, one time, in your single premium *fixed* annuity (CD annuity).

Now, you want an investment where you can add money monthly and still enjoy the benefits of an annuity. In that case, you want the flexible premium annuity. Usually, for as little as $100 a month, you can start dropping in money in this tax-deferred savings account—automatically.

The annuity company gives you a form to do an *automatic bank draft* from your checking account. It's a great way to supplement retirement funds and college-education funds. No sales charges. No monthly fees. No annual fees.

Income You Can't Outlive: The Immediate Annuity

"Income you can't outlive." You can't say that about a bank CD, bonds, stock, or a mutual fund. Here's the profile: No big growth needed or wanted, but you want big *income—now*. And you want this big income check, guaranteed, every month for as long as you (and your spouse) live.

So you "annuitize." You give your money to the annuity company and tell them to send you a check every month. When you're dead, the check goes to your spouse or other beneficiary. Additionally, when you're dead, a lump sum (or a part of it) can also pass on to your spouse or other beneficiary.

The risk to you is that you cannot access the principal as a lump sum while you're alive. The risk to the annuity company is that if you live a l-o-n-g time, they are obligated to pay the same benefit as long as you live. If they shell out more than the annuity is worth, that's tough. They dip into their resources and keep paying. You don't have to worry about interest rates or the stock market. The annuity keeps paying.

Note: it is *not necessary* to choose an immediate annuity in order to get income from your index annuity or CD annuity. You simply choose a systematic withdrawal plan from your index annuity or CD annuity. How does this work?

You have $100,000. You earned 7.50 percent or $7,500; $7,500 spread over 12 months is $625 a month. You tell the annuity company you want $625 a month, or $1,845 every three months, or $3,750 every six months, or $7,500 a year.

The principal stays in your name, under your control. The $625 keeps coming as long as you and your spouse live. You two die—the $100,000 goes to your kids or grandkids, or whomever you choose.

The downside of the systematic withdrawal plan is that the monthly income check may change *if* the interest rate changes in the second, third, or fourth year, and so on.

The first year you get 7.5 percent or $7,500, or $625 a month. The second year, the interest rate drops to 6.75 percent, which is $6,750 a year or $562 a month. The reverse of this is also true. Interest rates in the second year, third year, and so on rise to 8 percent. Now you get $8,000 a year, or $667 a month approximately.

With the immediate annuity, you won't worry about this. The income stays the same regardless of the economy, interest rates, or the stock market.

So the next question you have to answer is, "Which is best for me?" Well, that depends on you. Are you Joe Grow? Fred Fixed? Sam Save? Irene Income?

Let's look at each one and find out what suits you best.

Joe Grow

You have a lump sum of money. You want it to grow for several years, for long-term purposes (i.e., retirement, college education for kids or grandkids).

You want to ride the potential gains of the stock market. You know it fluctuates. You also know the *average annual return* of the market, as measured by the S&P 500, over 80 years has been an 8 to 12 percent return.[2] (Past performance is no guarantee of future results.)

You know that the market is like a person playing with a yo-yo while climbing a ladder. The yo-yo is going up and down, but the general direction is up.

You want stock market growth and you know the risk. Precisely because you know the risk, you want a bottom-line guarantee that you will *never* lose principal.

And you want the possibility of getting out income periodically. You want to know that, regardless of the market risk, your principal is safe and growing, guaranteed. You like the mix: When the market is up, you're up. When the market is down, you're still up.

If this is the case, you want the index annuity.

Fred Fixed

You've got a lump sum in a fixed, long-term account (like a CD) with a guaranteed interest rate. You want something as close to a CD as you can, but you need a better rate of return.

You look at the *fixed annuity*. You like its high rate of return, income liquidity, the fact that there's no probate, no current taxes, no exposure to lawsuits, and its overall safety.

You especially like the safety benefits of an annuity. You know that they are backed by insurance companies, and the one you have chosen is AA or better. You know that your three largest assets—your house, your life insurance policy, and your car—have *not* been entrusted to a credit union or bank, but to an insurance company. You have house *insurance,* life *insurance,* and car *insurance.*

You know that, in your state, your annuity and insurance holdings are probably covered by the Insurance Guaranty Corporation or a similar entity. So, you choose the fixed annuity for safety and stability.

Sam Save

You don't have a large sum, but you do have $100, $250, or $1,000 to save monthly. You want a safe, predictable return every month with the convenience of a monthly bank draft for $100, $250, or $1,000 with absolute safety.

You want the flexible premium annuity. It has the same safety and stability as a fixed annuity, but it's open-ended, meaning you can deposit money each month.

Irene Income

You want high, stable, predictable income—*now.* You want a steady, guaranteed income that you *cannot* outlive. The income will always be there, regardless of the stock market, interest rates, or the economy. Your goal is not to build a large estate. Your goal for this money is *immediate income.* Lots of it.

You want the immediate annuity.

Note: We deliberately did not include in this list variable annuities. Variable annuities do not meet the criteria of safety and stability. Variable annuities are, essentially, tax-deferred mutual funds, which suffer painful losses in down markets and extract high fees from the variable annuity owner. They can also create huge tax problems upon redemption.

CHAPTER SUMMARY

The Living Trust, the IBC, the ideal investment, the income annuity: These strategies really do provide peace of mind and deliver powerful protection.

I've shared them with millions in my radio audience. I've shared them with students in my investment classes and with thousands of clients in my private practice over the years. These strategies have worked for them. I am so confident that these are profitable and peace-of-mind strategies that I give my clients My

---

My Guarantee

I, Joe Green of ABC Brokerage Firm [or ABC Bank, Financial Company], friend, or advisor of Mr. or Mrs. Smith, guarantee that the recommendations that I make *will provide*:

➤ More income
➤ More growth
➤ More tax protection
➤ More estate protection

than the recommendations made by Dr. Gallagher.

If my recommendations do *not* provide:

➤ More income
➤ More growth
➤ More tax protection
➤ More estate protection

then I, Joe Green of ABC Brokerage Firm, pledge to personally make up the financial difference to Mr. or Mrs. Smith.

Signature: Joe Green, who works at ABC Brokerage Firm or ABC Bank.

Guarantee sheet and invite them to take it to their banker or broker with these instructions.

For example, my client's name is Mr. or Mrs. Smith. The broker or banker's name is Joe Green. (See "My Guarantee" box.)

ACTION STEPS

❑ Sit down with your spouse *and* your attorney and draft a living trust, so that your children and/or appointed beneficiaries will know what to do with your assets if you die or become disabled.

❑ Think long and hard before you decide on the person who will be your power of attorney. You may be putting yourself and your finances at risk!

❑ Explore the possibilities of an offshore corporation to potentially protect your assets and potentially protect yourself from lawsuits. Remember, a properly executed trust may give you the *benefits* of a power of attorney without exposing you to the *dangers* of a power of attorney.

❑ Figure out what your financial priorities are so you can determine what long-term investment plan is the best fit for you and your loved one(s).

❑ Once you've determined what your financial priorities are, sit down with an independent financial planner to put your plan into motion (i.e., fixed annuity, immediate annuity, trust, IBC, etc.).

CONCLUSION

With the right plan in place, you can be at ease in the event that tragedy strikes you or your loved one. Planning prevents panic.

But what happens if you don't plan? What do you do when the walls seem to close in on you and the pressure builds.

CHAPTER 5

The Pressure: When It's Too Late to Plan

The quickest way to send someone into depression is to seize his or her right to make choices about the course of his or her own life.
—Nursing Home Resident

Medicaid is not a solution. Medicaid is an admission that solutions were not sought and prevention was not practiced.

Medicaid is a default; it is one step up from living in an abandoned refrigerator box under the Interstate.

Five Ways to Take Care of Long-Term Care

Before we take a look at what happens when it's too late to plan for you or your loved one's long-term care, let's review the five ways to care for your loved ones. These loved ones are probably your parents who are now in their seventies or eighties, or perhaps your spouse who is in his seventies or eighties as you are. They are the ones who make up our greatest generation. They are the workers and homemakers who have devoted their lives to their families and their country. They came of age during the

Depression. They fought in World War II. They earnestly raised their children under the threat of thermonuclear war. They faithfully paid their taxes. They are America's solid, middle-class, patriotic, religious citizens who have worked, earned, and saved for decades.

But this greatest generation also has reached an age when many require a high level of care, and unfortunately, many did not do adequate planning. As a result, many of those who sacrificed so much for their families are now facing impoverishment because of long-term care expenses. How will you take care of them?

The first possibility is *self-care.* As we clearly saw in Chapter 2, self-care does not work. The family who tries to take care of a chronically ill family member becomes a chronically ill family. The second possibility is *private pay.* The average cost of a nursing home is $3,500 to $5,500 a month. Let's go with the median number and say $4,000. That's $48,000 a year per individual or $96,000 a year for a couple. In five years, that's nearly $500,000, a half-million dollars. I don't know too many people with a half-million dollars lying around in discretionary assets, and the costs are going up.

A third possibility for taking care of your loved ones is *Medicare.* With Medicare, full coverage for skilled nursing care is limited to 20 days. It pays only if an individual needing care is admitted following a three-day hospital stay and meets other Medicare requirements. Individuals with Medicare supplemental policies may have full coverage for up to an additional 80 days if they continue to meet the Medicare skilled nursing guidelines. After that, Medicare for skilled nursing care ends. (For those with no supplemental insurance, there is a per diem cost of about $3,000 per month.)

The fourth possibility is *long-term care (LTC) insurance.* That's the raging, torrential message of this book. Do long-term care planning, including buying long-term care insurance. Long-term care insurance covers home health care and assisted living, as well as nursing home care. Unfortunately, for seniors who are ill and cannot qualify for such insurance, *Medicaid*—our fifth and final possibility—may be their only option, which leads us to the heart of this chapter.

So let's say you blew it. You didn't plan and now your loved one needs a nursing home. What are your options now? The first that comes to mind is getting on Medicaid, or Medical Assistance. The truth of the matter is that there are two ways to be on Medicaid: (1) you plan for it or (2) you're pressured into it. Neither of these is a favorable scenario. Let's take a closer look at these two scenarios.

"I Plan to Be on Medicaid"

This option, "planning" to be on Medicaid, is an oxymoron. People surrender to Medicaid because they *haven't* planned. If you've got time to plan to be on Medicaid, then look at the other options more attractive than Medicaid. In fact, the previous chapter is passionately dedicated to those options. The reason I use the phrase "planning for Medicaid" is because that's exactly what your gentle and loquacious know-it-all friends will tell you. Which reminds me, the greatest threat to good long-term care planning is often hearsay—like saying that you can qualify for Medicaid by getting a divorce.

The recommendation from your friend goes like this. If you get a divorce, then instead of the government looking at the combined assets of your joint estate, the government will only be able to look at the assets of one of you, so you transfer assets out from one of the spouses to make that spouse look poor.

Let's face it: A couple who's been married 20, 30, 40 years will have to tell the judge why they want a divorce. In many states now, marital dispute arbitration is required before you go to divorce court. So that couple is going to have to lie about their reasons for divorce or tell the truth. If they tell the truth—"we wanted to qualify for Medicaid"—it's unlikely that a judge or arbitrator would grant a divorce. So the couple will likely resort to lying about why they are getting the divorce. If they lie to qualify for Medicaid, that is fraud.

So don't believe your buddy across the street who flippantly says, "Oh, you can just get a divorce and qualify for Medicaid."

This is yet another reason why adult children—those in their forties, fifties, or even sixties—will look at their aging mom and dad and say, "Wow, if they don't have long-term care insurance, we better get it for them." Mom and Dad may have a basket of reasons why they don't own long-term care insurance. Maybe they can't afford it or they think they'll never need it. You may chip in, say, $350 a month for long-term care insurance for both Mom and Dad. That monthly allotment is well worth it, because when Mom and Dad do need long-term care, they can receive care at home that will be paid for by an insurance policy, and it will not deplete the $500,000 in CDs, mutual funds, and so on, that they expected to pass on to their children.

As a child of an aging parent, it is important for you to advocate for your parents' best interests. After all, their Mr. or Ms. Know-It-All friend will be doing just the opposite. You know the type: He or she knows everything about how the federal government works, how to fix a leak, how to talk to a banker, how to choose a mutual fund, how to get a 4-percent reduction on the house you're planning to buy. They'll always tell you, "Well, my Uncle Louie did it this way," or "When that happened to my daddy, here's what we did," or "I've got a cousin over in Rochester. Here's how he took care of it." It's hearsay.

Remember this: Trying to do your own financial planning is like trying to do your own appendectomy. It's too close and it's too painful. The same is true of legal planning, which is what Medicaid requires.

The purpose of this section is to confront some of the obvious flaws in Mr. or Ms. Know-It-All's suggestions (i.e., how to hide money, so that you or your loved one will be eligible for Medicaid at the appropriate time):

Suggestion #1 "Transfer the money to your kids." There's a three-year look back in transferring any money. Also, you have to be able to show that transferring money to them was part of a normal pattern. If it looks like you were transferring money for the purposes of hiding it in order to qualify for Medicaid, that's fraud, and any Medicaid money will be denied. The government will force you to use all the "transferred money" before they will give you a penny of Medicaid money. You see, like Terri Schiavo in her final days, the Medicaid system is dry and starved. It frantically needs nourishment of cash and it's going to get it any way it can, including stopping all transfers.

Suggestion #2 "Transfer the money to a trust." A long time ago, there was something called a Medicaid Qualified Trust (an MQT). The idea there was to transfer money to a trust and then, because (technically) it's hands-off and arm's-length, you therefore qualified for Medicaid. But slipping money to you under the table, the trustee of your trust would give you whatever you needed whenever you needed it. No more, say the feds. Surprisingly, there are even professionals, like attorneys, who still recommend MQTs, not realizing they've been exposed and abolished.

MQTs are no longer viable! In fact, Medicaid will dissect any trust (even a so-called irrevocable trust) to determine if an applicant has any control or receives any benefits.

Suggestion #3 "Pay off your home or load it up with a lot of furnishings. They can't touch your home." Wrong! Because of the

Medicaid Estate Recovery Program (MERP)—which is sweeping across the country—they will seize your home—now or later. Later in this chapter, we discuss the specific arrangements that have to do with protecting your home.

To say that you plan to go on Medicaid is ludicrous because there may not be a Medicaid bed in your area. If there is, it may be in a place that you feel is dirty and dangerous. Furthermore, the Medicaid bed available for your mama may be in Buffalo, New York, and the Medicaid bed for Daddy might be in Albany. If you live in California, the Medicaid bed for Mama might be in Los Angeles and the Medicaid bed for Daddy might be in San Francisco. If there is no Medicaid bed available, and the line's getting longer and longer, do you come up with private pay or do you just wait until there's one available?

You don't want your loved one to plan for the Medicaid mess. There are legal reasons, practical reasons, quality of life reasons, and ethical reasons why you wouldn't—shouldn't—want to plan to go on Medicaid. From a legal standpoint, they can repossess your home later on. On the practical level, you'll be down on a list to get a bed, *if* there's one available. From a quality of life standpoint, if you got on a list to get care, it will likely be in a place where the care is subpar. We tackle the ethical reasons in depth at the end of the section on income and assets. Lastly, from a financial standpoint, can you live on $45 a month? That's the allowance the state gives you for all of your personal needs: soap, snacks, Kleenex, hair styling, laundry, cleaning, and so on.

"I Have No Choice But to Go on Medicaid"

Perhaps you didn't plan to be on Medicaid. But now, it's your only option. You ask yourself or your siblings and spouse, "What are we going to do with Mama! We've got to get her in a nursing home and ain't none of us got any money!" Sadly, this is the type of person whom I see in my office at least once a week. I get a panicked phone call to my radio show at least once a week.

Those of you who come to me for counseling are boiling with guilt, fear, and anger. You feel guilt because you feel you "should have done more to help Mama." You feel fear because none of you has the time or the money to care for Mom or Dad. Or you feel angry, an anger that boils like hot, frothing milk spilling over the pan, all over the stove. You're angry at God, at yourself, at your loved one, at the system. You're angry that you're under such pressure.

You don't know what to do with this guilt, fear, and anger, because you have an immediate crisis on hand. What's worse, you come face-to-face with the fact that the caseworker helping you has 500 other cases that she's taking care of, and you are definitely not her priority.

Because so many elders fail to plan for the costs of care, financial protection for their golden years and the small legacy they planned to leave to their families now seem ephemeral. Most must turn to Medicaid—a federal program funded by taxes that helps pay for long-term care. Yet many are shocked to discover how difficult it is to get Medicaid, how complex and intimidating the rules are, how stringent Medicaid's financial requirements are, how agency workers are restrained from assisting them for eligibility planning, and how they must "spend down" their assets to qualify for Medicaid.

Although you shouldn't plan to be on Medicaid, if your back's against the wall and no other options are available, a Medicaid plan of action is important. With the proper plan of action in place, no one has to be wiped out by a nursing home stay. Seniors facing long-term care should exercise this right. It is never too late to plan with the assistance of a Medicaid planning specialist who will help you gather the requisite personal and financial data.

Be sure to analyze your or your loved one's income and assets under the Medicaid rules; develop planning strategies for your particular case; and as needed, help with implementing plan options. There is no one size fits all solution, but a plan may be developed and implemented that will permit seniors to qualify for Medicaid while avoiding impoverishment and while conserving and protecting assets.

Eligibility for Medicaid

Exactly what is Medicaid? Medicaid is welfare, a program for the poor. If you can prove to the government that she's poor, they'll let you dump Mama in a nursing home and you won't pay a dime. Sounds like a good deal, but how do you convince the government that your loved one is poor?

First, you've got to know the ropes. You've got to know (1) the general provisions for Medicaid, (2) provisions for a single person, and (3) provisions for a married couple.

General Provisions

- Must be a U.S. citizen or an alien lawfully living in the United States.
- Must be over 65, blind, or disabled.
- Must have a medical necessity requiring nursing home care as determined by a physician.

Specific Provisions for a Single Person

Let's say the Medicaid candidate is your widowed mother. Your loved one must:

- Meet the income cap, meaning that she cannot receive more than $1,735 a month. (*Note:* The restrictions on this are rapidly changing. Some states are recommending that the income cap be lowered to $1,000 a month. So, if your loved one receives more than $1,000 a month, she may not qualify for Medicaid.)

- Have less than $2,000 in countable assets (checking, savings, etc.).
- Have less than $1,500 in cash value in an insurance policy, if she owns one.

She can maintain a home and all the normal furnishings that would go into a home. She can maintain the normal personal attire one normally possesses (clothes, jewelry, etc.). She can own one car, and there is no limitation on the value of that car. She can own a burial plot. She can own a term-life policy.

That's it.

There are other esoteric and technical exclusions such as possible ownership in a business. However, most people applying for Medicaid are not owners of businesses. Check with your local attorney to see if there are any other exclusions that may apply in your state.

Medicaid Planning for the Medicaid Spouse and Community Spouse

"Medicaid spouse" refers to the person going into the nursing home. This is the *Applicant*. In this case, let's assume it's the husband.

"Community spouse" refers to the person staying at home. Community spouse is sometimes referred to as the stay-at-home spouse.

- Maximum income cannot exceed $1,735 per month for the Medicaid spouse. Personal income for the community spouse is unlimited. Note: I said personal income, not joint income. This is the "Name on the Check" rule.

- In terms of assets, they cannot exceed $2,000 for the Medicaid spouse. The limit for the community spouse is $95,100. Note: In some states, the IRA of the community spouse can be seized if it exceeds this $95,100 limit.
  - The following exceptions apply and will not be counted toward the $2,000 or the $95,100 limit:

    Primary home.

    Personal jewelry purchased before the Medicaid application.

    Miscellaneous and customary household effects.

    Prepaid funeral.

    Burial account that does not exceed approximately $3,000.

    Term-life insurance policies.

    Business property, in some cases.

Countable assets are those assets that are included in the total amount of what you're eligible for or what you're allowed before you get on Medicaid. The noncountable are those assets *not* included in the total amount. Sometimes they are called "exempt assets," which means they're exempt from being counted.

You can also dump a bunch of cash into improvements on your current house. Some people think that you can hide this cash from the government by transferring lots of cash into the exempt column by way of expensive and cash-rich improvements to a house. Your strategy presumably is that when you die, your kids will get the house, sell it, and get all the money, which otherwise would have been seized by the government for Medicaid.

This won't work anymore. MERP is in. MERP means Medicaid Estate Recovery Program. All states now have MERP, which is federally mandated. This is another reason to look seriously at a trust if, indeed, one of your goals is to prevent your home or your parents' home from having a lien slapped on it by the government, which can result in eventual seizure.

The most important thing to keep in mind when making those transfers of cash is that at the time you make them, you must be in good health and have had no medical history of the illness that put you into a nursing home. Second, you must have established a pattern of making transfers of gifts—such as reducing the size of your estate—so at the time you made the transfer, you retained enough countable assets to pay for your then-anticipated medical expenses. If the transfer does not meet these criteria, Medicaid will consider it to be an attempt to "hide money."

Some important things to keep in mind about transfers: If you make any transfer within the look-back period, which is three years for a transfer to a person and five years for a transfer into a trust, *you must disclose those transfers to Medicaid.* If you hide the information about transfers, you are violating Medicaid procedures and may be guilty of fraud. Simply put, a look-back period is how far back Medicaid will go to see if you transferred any assets for less than fair market value in order to qualify for Medicaid. Assets that are transferred within the three-year period are considered countable transfers. The same holds true about money placed in trusts five years back from the time you filed your Medicaid application.

This means that if you wait for the three-year period or five-year period to expire, no law has been violated. The interpretation of this law, however, as it relates to you and your attempts to transfer money is uncertain. The moral implications of doing so, in my view, compel you to make financial arrangements ahead of time.

Most states consider it a legitimate transfer if (1) at the time when countable assets were given away, you were in good health with no medical history of the illness that put you into the nursing home, and (2) you showed a pattern of transferring assets.

One of the many ways the government is becoming more and

more aggressive in seizing assets is to look at the total assets of a couple, even if it's a second or third marriage, if there are prenuptial arrangements, and even if certain assets are in "sole and separate property accounts."

Let's look at John and Mary Smith, a fictional couple, to clearly illustrate this point. It is their second marriage and Mary has an inheritance from the first marriage of $500,000 and $50,000 in her own IRA. So as a couple, you say to the government regulators, "You can't include that when John has to go into a nursing home." But the government looks at the combined assets. The state looks at that and says, "We don't care if you have sole and separate property accounts. We don't care if you have a prenuptial agreement. We don't care if it's in retirement assets. That's our part of the estate."

At this point, you might ask, "Well, if Mary's got $500,000, why even apply for Medicaid?" That's the whole point. There are people who want to look poor on paper, so they can get Medicaid. That's why it is a bad idea to get on Medicaid. Mary's thinking—and John is in agreement—"Hey, that's your $500,000. You got that from your first marriage. You worked for that. We don't want to have to spend that just to be on Medicaid, so let's find a way to hide it." Getting a divorce is one way to hide it.

Are you familiar with the saying "The American people cannot sleep peacefully while Congress is in session!"? Nowhere does that ring more true than in the Medicaid rules. The rules change from state to state and almost month-to-month. Most importantly, the changes are ones that are not in your favor. They're getting stricter and stricter.

So, before you get involved in talking about Medicaid planning, make sure you talk with a certified elder law attorney. A good place to begin is to call your local bar association for a referral, or contact the National Academy of Elder Law Attorneys (NAELA). NAELA's address and web site are provided later in this chapter.

Okay, I've shown you some of the ways that you can legally transfer assets and legally restructure income (refer to Chapter 4), so that you or your loved one can qualify for Medicaid. These are legal, popular, and effective. The question that you want to raise as a member of the greatest generation known for sacrifice, virtue, and integrity is, "Is it ethical?"

Clearly there's an ethical issue with "cheating Uncle Sam for Mom and Dad." In the December 27, 2003, issue of *Newsweek*, writer Diana Conway said it right:[1]

> Every well-to-do senior who hides savings for the gain of his own family and seeks benefits meant for the needy weakens communal bonds. Have we become a nation of Scrooges, counting our own coins with little concern for others?
>
> I'm proud of my father. If my stepmother lives several years in her nursing home, or if he also needs long-term care, their life savings will run out. But he will leave me one thing of great value: an example of ethical behavior in an era when most people are out to grab everything they can for themselves.

In your case, maybe it's not an ethical issue. You really do need Medicaid for a variety of valid and legitimate reasons. Here's what's going to happen when you go to a certified elder law attorney. He or she is going to give you an expanded questionnaire and introduction to the Medicaid planning process. He or she will review your information and show you how you need to rearrange income and assets (if necessary) to qualify for Medicaid. If you go up to the Medicaid office, they'll give you a 23-page questionnaire. You see, Medicaid is not a piece of cake. You don't just show up and get in.

You show up at the Medicaid office. They look at your income and at your assets and they say, "You don't qualify for Medicaid." So, now you go visit with a qualified attorney who helps you shift the income and transfer the assets to make you appear poor on paper.

So how do you make yourself eligible if your assets exceed the maximum Medicaid limits? There are two primary ways. The first is to gift up to $5,600 a month. Only $2,800 of that would be discounted toward your eligibility. Also, you had better make sure you're telling the truth when you're stating your assets. You'll sign papers to give them the power to do a search on bank accounts, property, and so on. If you don't tell the truth for the purpose of qualifying for Medicaid, that's fraud.

Many folks think that they're restricted to giving away $12,000 a year. (These are 2006 figures. See Table 5.1 at the end of this chapter.) The truth is that you can give away as much money as you want to as many people as you want. And the money they receive is tax-free. A gift is a gift is a gift. But you, the donor, need to know about the potential consequences to you for excessive gifting. What this means is that you must understand the relationship between *estate* taxes and *gift* taxes.

Here it is:

1. You are Jane Generous, and you have an estate worth $5 million. You didn't realize your estate was that large until you added up everything: all property, jewelry, cars, IRAs, annuities, "big toys," and *life insurance*. Life insurance typically can add a whopping amount to the total value of your estate. You also have five children and five grandchildren.

2. Each individual is "allowed" (Isn't it nice that Big Government gives us permission to manage some of our own money?) to give away $12,000 per year, per recipient. You are also allowed a *unified tax credit* of $2 for estate tax purposes.

3. So, you, Jane Generous, give $12,000 away each year to each of your children and grandchildren. That's $12,000

to a total of ten recipients for a grand total of $120,000 a year. You now have five children and five grandchildren who are very grateful children and grandchildren . . . or at least they should be.

4. You do this generous gifting for eight years. That's a total of $960,000 given away ($120 × 8 = $960,000).

5. You die. No surprises here.

6. Your estate of $5 million is worth, for estate tax purposes, $3 million. Big Government allows you a unified tax credit of $2 million . . . remember? The total gifts of $960,000 did not affect your unified tax credit.

7. Switch scenes: You are now Jane *Super-Generous*. You now give away $150,000 a year every year for eight years.

8. That's a total of $1.2 million given away ($150 × 8 = $1.2 million).

9. You die.

10. Remember that unified tax credit of $2 million that you or your heirs thought you would get? It's gone, in part. It's been reduced by $200,000, because you went $200,000 *over* the allowable gift limit of $1 million. This reduction is essentially what is called the *gift tax*.

    So . . . how did Big Government "getcha" on this one? You were $200,000 over the gift limit, so they subtracted the $200,000 from your $2 million unified tax credit. Now your unified tax credit is only $1.8 million ($2 million − $200,000 = $1.8 million).

11. Your estate of $5 million, upon your death, is now subject to estate taxes on $3.2 million. $5 million minus the new and reduced unified tax credit of $1.8 million equals $3.2 million. Your heirs have to pay estate taxes on $3.2 million.

As a couple, how do you pass on money to others? There are a couple of ways. You can set up a "special trust," with detailed stipulations that you yourself specify. For example, you can set up a trust for A or a trust for B, and so on. These are A-B trusts. There are also complex strategies for Advanced Charitable Gifting, Family Limited Partnerships, and Private Foundations. These are beyond the scope of this book. See your local counsel and your local tax advisor.

How about transferring funds between spouses? How about annuities? Some financial planners take the position—again, check with a local attorney—that an immediate annuity for husband or wife will allow you to take countable assets and transfer them into noncountable. For example, let's say you have $80,000 that you want to preserve. Right now, it's in the countable asset column. The community spouse (otherwise known as the stay-at-home spouse) takes that $80,000 and buys an immediate annuity that generates $700 a month. The $80,000 is now gone from the assets column (unable to be seized by Medicaid) and has been transformed into income of $700 a month. Remember, income for the community spouse has no limits and cannot be seized.

As pointed out earlier, other ways to spend down assets to qualify for Medicaid are upgrading a house, or buying an automobile, or purchasing burial plots for yourself and your spouse. You can also gift $5,600 a month to your spouse or children. In addition, you can take advantage of a supplemental needs trust that could be used for someone's special needs, like a disabled child.

What happens to the spouse who refuses to give up his or her assets? If the community spouse refuses to cooperate, Medicaid *must* qualify the applicant immediately. However, Medicaid will use the spouse's assets to determine eligibility and the penalty period. And, as mentioned earlier, failure to fully disclose the Medicaid spouse's assets *or the community spouse's assets* is fraud.

How about option two, the Medicaid qualified annuity? I touched on this briefly earlier. It's an option that has been misrepresented by many insurance salespeople. They give you the impression that if you put the money into annuities, somehow you are protected from reporting it for eligibility. Not so.

Let's take the case of the single person. You have $100,000. You want to take that out of the assets column. The only way to do that is to put it into the income column. You buy a life-only immediate annuity and it starts generating $760 a month. That would make you the annuitant, or the person entitled to receive the benefits from an annuity.

The problem with that is that it makes your income flow sky-rocket, and as we mentioned before, the income limit for a single individual cannot exceed $1,735 *monthly* to qualify for Medicaid. Anything over that amount would go into a Miller trust, which we discuss in more detail later in this chapter. The only purpose of this trust is to resolve the income cap issue for Medicaid applicants—no more, no less. Its proceeds can be used only for long-term/nursing home care.

The point is, if you're trying to protect $100,000 from being used for your nursing home care—as a single person—it's not going to happen. Income shifting and annuity strategies seem to work only with married couples.

If done right, the Medicaid-qualified immediate annuity will work and is allowable in the case of a married couple. The first thing to remember, however, is that the Medicaid spouse (the one applying for Medicaid) usually cannot use an immediate annuity to protect the $100,000. This $100,000 is in the assets column of the Medicaid spouse and is therefore not allowable: too much money. If the $100,000 is transferred via an immediate annuity into $760-a-month income for the Medicaid spouse, that is also not allowable, because it adds too much income to the income column for this Medicaid spouse. Again, too much money.

So what does this couple do?

The community spouse (the stay-at-home spouse) cannot have more than $95,000 in assets *but can have unlimited income*, so in this case we have the community spouse take the $100,000 and put that into an immediate annuity. We now have $760 a month being generated for income for the community spouse, and the community spouse can have all the income she wants.

There is one exception to this rule that would allow the Medicaid spouse to use a Medicaid-qualified annuity. If he has assets of, say, $100,000, he (the Medicaid spouse) can buy an immediate annuity. He's the annuitant. The owner is his wife, and the beneficiary in that case has to be the state. In this scenario, the wife as owner and as the community spouse can receive the income from this annuity with no limitations, but upon death, the final recipient of beneficiary proceeds is the state. The state wants to recover assets that it used to provide Medicaid care for that Medicaid spouse.

The Miller Trust

You're the Medicaid spouse, and your income is $2,000 a month. Remember, the income cap is $1,735. You would take $300 a month and send it to your Miller trust. The Miller trust sends that $300 to the Medicaid nursing home. You are still paying for it, but technically, on paper, you fall below the monthly income cap. That's how you qualify for Medicaid.

To do this right, you absolutely need a qualified Medicaid attorney, not a CPA, not a friend from church, not a helpful relative. To repeat, *you need a qualified Medicaid attorney*. An attorney who practices general law probably can't do it, and even one who identifies himself or herself generically as an elder law attorney may not be able to do it. You need to have somebody who really knows the ropes of the Medicaid system. They're hard to find and they're expensive, because they're in such demand. Having said that, if you get the right person it will be worth it, because he or she can save you a lot of headaches and a lot of money.

If you need help beyond the scope of this book, you can write me at the address mentioned on page 209, and I will help you find a qualified attorney or two in your area.

Okay, you've used the Miller trust to meet the income eligibility requirement. What about the assets? You're the community spouse, and if the total of all your resources is between $18,000 and $90,000, that is the amount you get to keep. Anything above that must be spent on your spouse's care before he's eligible for Medicaid. So if you have resources totaling, say, $200,000, then $105,000 must be spent down in order to keep you below the $95,000 cap. Presumably this extra amount of assets, this $105,000 can go into the Miller trust, which will then pass it on to the state to help subsidize the Medicaid costs for your husband, the Medicaid spouse.

Protecting Your Home, Your Very Special Asset

Married Couples

It should be a slam dunk for a married couple to protect their home, because the home is owned by both of them. Say you're the community spouse (the wife), and your husband is the Medicaid patient. He's applying for Medicaid, and the ownership of the home automatically transfers to you, because, after all, it has always been a home owned by you jointly. You, the community spouse, get to stay in the home forever.

When your husband dies, you are now single, and the rules

applying to ownership of a home by a single person then kick in. We'll discuss those later. But there are potentially two dangers with the ownership of a home by a married couple. What if you don't live in a community property state? Check with your attorney, *right now*, to confirm if you are in a community property state, and if you are not, find out how that would potentially affect Medicaid eligibility in the future.

Here's another danger (and I've seen this happen with couples). You're in a second marriage. Your husband owns the house, and you have a will (meaning that the estate goes through probate). Your husband goes into a nursing home paid for by Medicaid. He dies. Because of the Medicaid Estate Recovery Program (MERP), the state looks at all the probated assets, which include your house. Presumably, the state can then, upon your husband's death, seize the house and sell it as a probated asset to recover the costs of providing Medicaid for your husband. However, in some states, the recovery process will only begin at the death of both spouses. Check with local counsel, and as I've pleaded throughout this book, get long-term care insurance or have Bill Gates-type resources to make sure that neither you nor your husband have to go on Medicaid *ever*.

Single Persons

A single person who owns a home can transfer it to the following classes of people without triggering an ineligibility period:

- A sibling who has had an equity interest in the property for at least one year.
- A child who is a minor and/or is blind or disabled.
- A child who has lived in the home for at least two years prior to his or her parent's entry into a nursing home and who has provided a level of care.

Transfer Penalty Exceptions

When you transfer your home, Medicaid disqualifies you from eligibility for benefits except in certain cases. A single person or married couple can transfer a house to:

- A child who is blind, disabled, or under 21 years of age.
- A sibling who owns a share of the home and has resided there for at least one year before the co-holder goes into the nursing home.
- A child (of any age) who has resided in the home for at least two years before the parent's institutionalization, and can show that he has cared for the parent at home.
- Anyone at any time, as long as it is for fair market value. If indeed it is a transfer for "fair market value," this is a transfer by deed and is essentially a *sale*. In that case, it is a countable asset. If it is a transfer by gift, then this triggers a look-back for the penalty period in order to be a noncountable asset.
- Anyone, provided the purpose of the transfer is not to qualify for Medicaid. For example, a person gives his house to his children while healthy for the purpose of avoiding probate or estate taxes. Later, he is permanently disabled in an accident and is forced to go into a nursing home within three years of making the transfer. This transfer would probably not disqualify him from Medicaid.

One last possibility: Even though the transfer of a house would ordinarily disqualify a person for Medicaid, he may still receive benefits if he can show that he would suffer undue hardship by not being granted benefits. This alternative is rarely accepted by Medicaid.

Additional Protection for Your Home

A more radical option to protect your home is to give it away outright. However, the first and most obvious disadvantage of doing so is that it leaves you no control. Second, you sacrifice the one-time exemption from capital gains in the sale of your home. According to the IRS, this stipulates that as long as you lived in your primary residence for two of the past five years leading up the sale of the property, you are entitled to sell and keep a portion of the proceeds—up to $250,000 for a single individual and $500,000 for a married couple—tax free. Third, you pass to the receiver greater capital gains tax liability.

A more viable option you may entertain is to give away your home with a life estate. By doing so, you still keep the interest in the property for the remainder of your life. The last alternative to protecting your home is to place it in a trust. Some authorities believe the only way that you can protect your home is to have an income-only trust. This type of trust is irrevocable and is useful to preserve assets for future generations (i.e., children, grandchildren, etc.).

I know. You'll have friends and neighbors tell you they know somebody who hid their money by doing this and this and this. These are the Joe and Jane Know-It-Alls. They know all about real estate, cars, the IRS, stocks, wills and trusts, and oil and gas. And they're just as broke as you, or just as confused as you. I urge you to ignore them and go to reliable sources.

Summary

The big problem with Medicaid is that you lose your control, money, independence, and maybe proximity to your family. Don't make it worse by getting bad advice.

And you'd better be really broke in order to get Medicaid, because efforts are under way to make you sell your house now, to make you cash in everything now in order to put in your substantial portion before Medicaid kicks in. Forget about the old ways to "hide your money."

Is There Protection Against Medicaid Costs?[2]

As you have learned, the "community spouse resource limits" established by Medicaid are insufficient in today's world. And, the Medicaid qualification process can be very complex, especially when it comes to protecting the community spouse. In order to maintain that treasured protection, some couples have discovered that if the community spouse (the wife, let's say) had the power of attorney which contained gifting provisions for the Medicaid spouse (the husband), then substantial and legitimate gifting could have been done before the Medicaid qualification period began.

How About Inherited Money?

Let's say the husband receives inherited money from a generous aunt at about the same time he needs Medicaid. Can he disclaim his share of the inheritance? The answer is no, because by disclaiming his share of the inheritance, the husband has in effect made a gift and will be disqualified from Medicaid benefits for a number of months—calculated by dividing $100,000 by the average monthly private pay nursing home rate in your state. To further compound this problem, by making a disclaimer, the amount the husband would have received would be put back into the estate and, depending on the wording of the inheritance will, you, the community spouse, may or may not benefit from it. And to make matters worse, if he disclaims, you would be required to pay for his care and not have the money with which to do it. If he receives the inheritance, you will be required to use up his share, and at requalification if you are again over the spousal limit, you will be required to spend your share also.

Had your husband's aunt changed her generous will and left his share in a special needs trust for him, or had she left the total $100,000 to you, he would not have been disqualified.

As you can see, it's getting tougher and tougher to hide money from the government in order to qualify for Medicaid. You just may have to suck it up and realize that you've got to spend your money first and maybe sell off your property before you qualify for Medicaid. The trend is clear. Estate recovery is coming, and it's coming aggressively, meaning that even if you transferred money to a trust five years ago, that five-year line will be erased.

Moreover, even if you transferred money to your children three years ago, that three-year line will be erased, and anything that was in your name will be seized in order to reimburse the government for its Medicaid expenses or in order to make you cough up and pay first before Medicaid kicks in. Again, if that is a real concern of yours, then that's another reason to possibly look at an international business corporation where assets cannot be found. Again, check with your local attorney, because you cannot do anything that even begins to look like you're defrauding the government. You go to jail for that and so does the lawyer, financial planner, CPA, or insurance agent who may help you do it.

Remember, when it comes time, the application for your loved one may not be at all like those we've discussed earlier or like the profile because "whenever Congress is in session, the American people cannot sleep peacefully."

Like earth plates scraping and sliding against each other miles below the surface and later bursting into a hot volcanic spray, Congressional attitudes are scraping and sliding against each other, ready to burst into a volcanic spray of more penalties against people who try to hide money from Medicaid.

At this writing, there is a three-year look-back on transferring to children. Furthermore, you may transfer to your children, and it's gone. "Transfer" means you allow him or her to have irreversible control and ownership. The assets are under his or her name and Social Security number. There are lots of problems with this approach. For example, what happens if your son or daughter

- Dies? Who's going to get the money, and is that person trustworthy? You have all the same potential problems with that secondary trustee as you potentially do with your son or daughter.
- Is disabled? Ditto. Same problems as with your son or daughter dying.
- Is sued? If your child is sued, Medicaid will go after the assets in the trust. At this point, we're talking about a *revocable* living trust. There is such a thing as an *irrevocable* living trust.
- Marries a liar or a crook? He marries someone who's had earlier problems with the IRS. The IRS comes after her, which means it comes after your son or daughter, which means it comes after all the assets in that trust.

  A trust does not provide legal protection, nor does it provide tax protection. Furthermore, that person he marries finds a way into his heart and wallet and gets her name on the trust and on the checking account, so it looks like everything is community property. They divorce, and she invades those assets.

- Becomes greedy and desperate? "Not me. Never happen to my kids. My kids are perfect." If you believe that there can never be any financial misunderstanding in your family, or that assets cannot disappear unbeknownst to you into some other accounts—either accidentally or deliberately—if you believe all that, then I have in my back pocket the deed to the Empire State Building, which I'll sell to you today for $1,000.

Your answer to all these five objections is, "Well, I'll set it up so I can get it back anytime I want!" Okay, now you have hands-on access to it, which means you won't qualify for Medicaid.

The other problem that relates to transferring it to a child or transferring it to a trust is the state's increasing aggression in "estate recovery." Right now, the house (which is worth, let's say, $100,000) is protected from seizure.

So you go on Medicaid. Previously, the house had been left alone. It was sold and the $100,000 proceeds were divided according to the will. Not anymore. You go on Medicaid, and that house you left that was worth $100,000, $200,000, $300,000, upon your death is forcibly sold by the government. They seize the house, sell it, and recover the assets to repay themselves for what they paid on your behalf for your Medicaid help.

Now, if they'll do it for the house, then they'll do it for other assets. In other words, there's nothing sacred about having a three-year look-back period for children. Watch out! All the assets, the CDs, mutual funds, and automobiles you transferred to your child, the regulators will eventually come after when you're dead, to repay themselves for Medicaid costs.

A transfer to a trust with a five-year look-back period—whose trust? Is it revocable or irrevocable? If it's a revocable trust, it's in your name with your Social Security number. If it's in your name with your Social Security number, then you have access to it. If you have access to it, you don't qualify for Medicaid. So you transfer it to a trust in somebody else's name, like your son's. Now we have his name, your son's name. Now you have all the problems previously outlined.

Okay, so then you decide to transfer the funds to an annuity. That is a shooting from the hip glib solution by many insurance salespeople or self-appointed financial planners. A "Medicaid annuity" is a very specialized type of annuity, not just any annuity. It must have prior approval because it is basically one that requires that the primary beneficiary be the government. The idea of a Medicaid annuity is this: When you fill out a Medicaid application, there are two categories, income and assets.

Assets must meet certain minimum criteria. If you meet them, there are ways to protect your assets from lawyers and from predators, but they have nothing to do directly with Medicaid qualifications. The strategies used are a Nevada corporation or an offshore corporation (also known as an international offshore corporation). I am not a lawyer, but I can read and I know the general parameters of how they work.

By the way, they are perfectly legal. They've received a notorious reputation because allegedly they're used by drug dealers and porno dealers to skim off money and hide profits. If that's your purpose, shut this book and go directly to jail.

Here's how it works. You, John Doe, set up a Nevada corporation, and you call it My Safe Money, Inc. Now, My Safe Money, Inc., is incorporated in the State of Nevada. It has a tax ID number that is not attached to you. There are companies in Nevada that specialize in doing this, so all tax ID numbers are attached to that company. Now that company works for you, but your name is not on any documents. So if somebody sues you, John Doe, and you have money in My Safe Money, Inc., with a different tax ID number, then you technically do not have direct access to it, and they can't get to that money because they can't find it.

This is not a tax avoidance or a tax evasion strategy nor is it a strategy to avoid paying your rightful obligations. This is a strategy to hide your money from the greedy lawyers or unscrupulous creditors who are after you. This is a strategy to protect yourself from frivolous litigation.

You heard the story about the couple who were on vacation. During their vacation, a burglar broke into their house and in casing out the garage, got himself locked in. The garage did not have any windows, the kitchen door was locked, and he couldn't get back into the kitchen. In the garage was a bag of dog biscuits and a case of warm Pepsi. He kept himself alive by munching on dog biscuits and drinking Pepsi. When the couple returned, he sued the couple for emotional and physical distress, and he won a judgment of $5,000. Cases go on and on and on about innocent people who have been sued successfully. If a lawyer cannot find your assets, he will not sue you.

Here's how it works. You're a lawyer, and I think I have a case against Dr. Brown. Unbeknownst to me, Dr. Brown has set up a Nevada corporation for all of his assets. He has allegedly done something wrong to me. I go to you, and I say, "I want to sue Dr. Brown," and you say, "Sure, let's sue him. Let's sue his wife, and just sign this form. I will get 40 percent of whatever I recover." So, he goes to the Internet, to check out what Dr. Brown has. We know Dr. Brown has a house, but the house is not in his name.

The lawyer can't find anything beyond $1,000 in a checking account. So the lawyer says, "If you want me to sue, I'm going to need a $10,000 retainer, and I'll bill you regularly as I continue the suit." You're not going to do it. You were hoping all along that you could file a suit and get a large judgment, and the lawyer would get his money out of that.

There is a latent suspicion or hostility toward citizens who ostensibly set up any device for the purpose of paying for Medicaid. I am not saying that you eschew your ethical and legal responsibilities to pay for your own long-term care. Actually, this matter's already been taken care of, because there's still the three-year look-back. If you had set up a Nevada or offshore corporation, there still would be a three- to five-year look-back to seize those assets. So if you plan to use this to protect your assets, it must be done prior to the look-back period, or there is no protection.

Introduction to the Medicaid Mess

The Medicaid program is running out of money. So, when it's your turn and they go broke, they'll either kick you out of your bed or deny you a bed outright.

Medicaid payments to a nursing home are less than private payments you give out-of-pocket or from your long-term care insurance policy. So, if Medicaid payments are for the welfare patients, who do you think gets the inferior care in nursing homes?

"Say it ain't so, Doc!" I know better. Many of my clients are nurses and other health care workers. They relate documented stories of Medicaid patients being isolated, forgotten, and denied.

With Medicaid, you have no choice where you will live. Your Medicaid bed can be *anywhere* in your state. What's worse is that Medicaid strips you of your privacy, dignity, and freedom.

The Grandma Goes to Jail regulations are still in effect! If you or a professional you work with knows you have sufficient assets to pay for long-term care, yet proceeds to hide those assets, so that you look poor on paper and therefore can qualify for Medicaid, that person (or persons) can be fined or jailed.

Medicaid will first force you to use those "transferred assets" (which you refused to disclose), and then Medicaid may slap you with a fine or a charge of fraud.

The Medicaid application process is long, confusing, and potentially dangerous. Do it wrong, and someone gets denied, cheated, and/or goes to jail. The sadder part is that when your money runs out and you go on Medicaid, they kick you out because your facility does not have a Medicaid bed. That's traumatic.

The moral of this story: You should have planned long ago to have long-term care insurance or abundant assets to pay for long-term care. If it's too late for you, get the services of an elder law attorney. If you don't know where to start, I suggest you go to: http://www.naela.com (the National Academy of Elder Law Attorneys' web site). NAELA is located at 1604 North Country Club Road, Tucson, AZ 85716 (520-881-4005).

Medicaid Frequently Asked Questions

Applying for Medicaid is a laborious process. Undoubtedly, you will have questions. The following section is dedicated to frequently asked questions about Medicaid. Hopefully, it will serve as a good reference point/guide if you find yourself needing to apply for Medicaid.

Is there any protection against Medicaid costs? Let my client speak for herself.

My husband suffered a stroke at age 62. Five years later, he was diagnosed with Alzheimer's disease. I cared for him at home until my own health began to deteriorate. With our son's help, I placed my husband in a nursing facility and paid more than $5,000 monthly for three years by using my husband's Social Security and pension (which totaled $2,000 per month) and money drawn from his 401(k).

As our resources dwindled, I finally went to our state Medicaid office and was told that before my husband could qualify for assistance, I had to spend his assets down to $2,000, including his 401(k). I could keep our house and car, but had to reduce my countable assets to less than $60,000, which is the state minimum for community spouses. So, for the next 15 months, I paid more than $5,500 per month for his care to reduce our assets to an acceptable level. He then qualified for Medicaid benefits, but my standard of living was severely diminished because we had planned to use the income from the assets, which are now spent.

I had to stop paying the premiums on his life insurance because I could not afford them.

Then, not six months later, his 97-year-old aunt died and, quite unexpectedly, left him $100,000 and me $60,000. I thought this was lucky, but the Medicaid official said that as soon as my husband was entitled to receive his share of the inheritance, he would be disqualified for Medicaid and would have to go back on private pay until the entire $100,000 was spent. I checked with an estate lawyer who told me that I could use my husband's power of attorney to disclaim his share of the inheritance, and that the estate could just shift his share into my name—which does not sound exactly right. I am confused, Dr. Gallagher, and wish I had met you several years ago.

How does one qualify for Medicaid long-term nursing home benefits? In order to qualify for Medicaid, an applicant must: (1) be a U.S. citizen or an alien lawfully living in the United States; (2) be over 65, disabled or blind; (3) have a "medical necessity" requiring skilled nursing care; (4) meet the income cap (no more than $1,735 monthly as of 2005); and (5) have only limited assets.

If I qualify for Medicaid, can I get into any nursing home? Not all nursing homes accept Medicaid benefits. Of those nursing homes that do, the nursing home may only accept a limited number of Medicaid recipients. Additionally, the Medicaid bed generally is in a semiprivate room.

What happens if my spouse, who's the applicant, receives $1,000 per month in income, and I receive $1,735 or even $3,000 per month in income? The applicant will not have a problem with the income cap because he is receiving less than $1,737 per month. The Medicaid agency looks only at the applicant's income for Medicaid eligibility. If a couple is receiving rental payments from a lease of their land or are receiving note payments, the Medicaid agency will consider that the income goes to the spouse whose name is on the check.

What if I or my loved one qualify for Medicaid long-term nursing home care, but the income exceeds the income cap? If the applicant otherwise qualifies for Medicaid long-term nursing home benefits, the applicant (or the applicant's spouse or duly appointed agent) may create a qualified income trust or Miller trust. This trust allows the applicant to transfer his/her income into the trust and then qualify for Medicaid long-term nursing home care benefits.

Among other provisions, the trust must provide that upon the death of the beneficiary/applicant, the state will be reimbursed for all expenditures made on the applicant's behalf. If the applicant is married, the benefits will be paid out of the trust as follows:

- A $45 allowance to the beneficiary and/or applicant and any guardian fees will be paid.
- An allowance will be paid to the at-home spouse (referred to as the "community spouse") in order to bring the com-

munity spouse's income up to $2,377.50 (the minimum monthly maintenance needs allowance for a community spouse as of 2005), and there may be an allowance provided for dependents living at home.

- If there are any "incurred medical expenses," such as supplemental (Medigap) medical insurance premiums and costs of medical care not covered but approved by Medicaid, those amounts can be paid out of the trust.
- "Applied income" will be paid to the nursing home.
- Any remaining income can be disbursed for the beneficiary/applicant's supplemental needs but, practically speaking, seldom will there be any funds left after payment of the applied income.

If the applicant is not married, the spousal allowance will be eliminated.

Can I transfer my assets into a Miller trust to protect them? No. A Miller trust is used *only* to overcome the income cap issue. A Miller trust is *not* a trust used to protect assets (resources).

What are the limited nonexempt assets that I as an unmarried individual can own and still qualify for Medicaid? To qualify for Medicaid, an unmarried individual's countable resources (assets) cannot exceed $2,000.

What are the limited nonexempt assets that I and my spouse can own and either one or both of us still qualify for Medicaid? If both spouses are applying for long-term nursing home benefits, then their combined countable resources generally cannot exceed $3,000. If only one spouse is applying for Medicaid benefits, the community spouse will keep more than $2,000 in assets.

When the Medicaid application is completed, all available nonexempt resources of both spouses will be counted as resources, whether the property is classified as community or separate. One-half of the couple's resources will be set aside for the spouse not applying for Medicaid benefits, with a minimum set aside amount of $19,020 (as of 2005) and a maximum of $95,100 (as of 2005).

There may be ways in which to increase the maximum amount that can be set aside for the spouse staying at home, but the strategies can be complex and should be discussed with your attorney.

What if I am told that I have to spend down resources before I or my spouse qualifies for Medicaid? Should I spend down before I fill out an application for Medicaid or after the application is made? Spending down before or after the application is not the key. The Medicaid agency gives you credit for all monies spent after you enter a medical facility and ultimately stay for 30 days or more. For example, Wife has a stroke and goes into the hospital in September. On October 4, she is moved into a nursing facility and continues to reside there. Husband completes the application for Medicaid benefits for her in December. The Medicaid agency will determine what their assets were on September 1 and again on December 1 to see if they have already spent funds to meet any spend down.

When only one spouse is applying for Medicaid, it is best to spend down *after* the Medicaid application is filed. This is generally after a person goes into a nursing home. You can actually be in a nursing home during the process while you're spending down the assets, except during that time, you're paying for it yourself. Then when you can document that it's all been paid out, all your private resources are exhausted. Then you're already in there, you're already in your bed, and then Medicaid picks it up. You've got to make sure, though, that from the get-go, you're in a Medicaid bed, so after the pay runs out, they don't kick you out until a Medicaid bed becomes available or move you halfway across the state.

Will all of my or my loved one's resources or assets be counted when determining Medicaid eligibility? No. The following assets are exempt from being included as a resource:

- The applicant's principal residence.
- A burial plot held for the applicant or the applicant's family.
- Term or burial insurance, if it has no cash value.
- Identifiable burial funds in the amount of $1,500 or a pre-paid irrevocable burial contract regardless of value.
- If there is a community spouse, one automobile is exempt, regardless of value. If the applicant has no community spouse, then one automobile of unlimited value can be owned.
- Household goods and personal effects have no limit on their value.
- Life insurance policies owned by the applicant with a face value of $1,500 or less.
- Livestock that is held for business purposes or for consumption.
- Business property essential for self-support.
- Nonbusiness property valued at up to $6,000, essential for self-support (generally mineral interests).

If I go into a nursing home, will I have to sell my homestead and spend the money before I qualify for Medicaid long-term nursing home benefits? No, you do not need to sell your homestead and spend the money in order to qualify for Medicaid. The Medicaid agency considers your homestead an exempt asset and therefore will not include it when determining your eligibility.

What happens if both my spouse and I go into a nursing home permanently? Will we have to sell our home or will the State place a lien on our home and foreclose on that lien? Again, you should not have to sell your homestead even if you go into a nursing home to live out your life. The State does not have the ability to place a lien on the homestead.

Can I give away some of my assets to qualify for Medicaid? Generally, no. If a nursing home applicant makes a transfer of resources for less than fair market value (a gift) in order to qualify for Medicaid benefits, the applicant will be penalized for the gift by being ineligible for Medicaid benefits for a calculated period of time (the transfer penalty).

The Medicaid agency has determined that the average private pay cost for nursing home care is $2,908 (for September 1, 2003 through August 31, 2005). To determine the number of months of ineligibility for any gift, the Medicaid agency will divide the amount of the gift by $2,908 and drop any remainder. If a gift is made, the presumption is that it was made in order to qualify for Medicaid benefits. The applicant would have to prove that the gift was made for a totally different reason, which is a very difficult burden of proof.

Under federal and state law, the Medicaid agency can look back for 36 months to determine if an individual made an outright gift. Additionally, the look-back period for a transfer into a trust is generally 60 months.

Can I transfer all of my assets into a trust and then apply for and qualify for Medicaid long-term nursing home benefits? Although its specific provisions vary from state to state, Congress does allow a *disabled* person under the age of 65 to transfer assets to a supplemental needs trust without transfer penalties. A supplemental needs trust that is created by (signed by) a parent, a grandparent, a guardian, or a judge who holds the assets of a disabled applicant who is under 65 is also exempt from the transfer penalties. Both of these trusts require that upon the death of the applicant/beneficiary, all Medicaid expenditures are paid back to the State out of the remaining trust funds. These trusts are generally irrevocable.

When spouses transfer their assets into a living trust, the Medicaid agency takes the position that as long as the trust is revocable, it is as if the parties still owned the assets because the parties can revoke the trust at any time and get their assets back. There is no transfer penalty as long as the spouses can recover the property from the trust. However, when the first spouse dies, if the trust requires that the deceased spouse's property must pass into a trust for the surviving spouse, such a transfer could result in a Medicaid disqualifying transfer penalty applied against the surviving spouse (even if the decedent's trust for the surviving spouse had supplemental needs language). These rules are complex, so before creating a trust with the intent of applying for Medicaid, a person should contact a certified elder law attorney.

Can I put my assets in an annuity (sometimes referred to as a Medicaid annuity) and protect them from Medicaid scrutiny? The answer is, most often, no. An annuity that allows a person to access the cash assets (similar to a savings account) is a countable asset. If the annuity is annuitized, it will be paying monthly payments and the fund cannot be cashed out.

The rules governing the Medicaid program require the Medicaid recipient to name their state of residence as the primary beneficiary so that on the death of the Medicaid recipient, any funds remaining in the annuity will be used to reimburse the State. A spouse can purchase a single premium immediate annuity (a stream of payments, not a savings account) without penalty. There is no requirement that the State receive the remaining funds upon the spouse's death. However, if the spouse ever wants to obtain Medicaid assistance, the State would have to be named the primary beneficiary or the spouse would be disqualified because of the existence of the annuity.

Because an annuity contract could contain significant surrender penalties (over and above the tax issues), a person should contact a certified elder law attorney to determine the pros and cons of investing in annuities.

I have a power of attorney for my loved one. Can I make small gifts in anticipation of applying for Medicaid benefits? As noted, gifting can create a period of ineligibility for Medicaid long-term care benefits. However, with proper legal guidance, one might possibly make small gifts. I advise against gifting for a number of reasons, including but not limited to:

1. The applicant cannot demand the return of the money, if needed (it was a gift, so the money is gone).
2. The donee (person receiving the gift) may intend to keep the money and use it for the applicant, but what if the donee:
   - Dies before the applicant?
   - Has creditors who can get the gift in payment of the donee's debt?
   - Has a spouse who spends the gift?
   - Spends the gift anyway?

While it is risky to make gifts, there are ways to accomplish a plan of gifting, but this plan should only be undertaken with the supervision of a certified elder law attorney.

What could happen if I use a power of attorney to make gifts of an elderly person's funds and someone complains? In most states, there is a law that says: " 'Exploitation' means the illegal or improper act or process of a caretaker, family member, or other individual who has an ongoing relationship with the elderly or disabled person using the resources of an elderly or disabled person for monetary or personal benefit, profit, or gain without the informed consent of the elderly or disabled person."—Texas Human Resources Code §48.002(3).

If Adult Protective Services (APS) finds that a person used a power of attorney (or any other means) to transfer the applicant's money for the benefit, profit, or personal gain of someone else (made a gift) without the applicant's informed consent, then APS could find that the person making the transfer has *exploited* the applicant. Transfer of funds as small as $1,500 can result in a state jail felony charge. Therefore, it is imperative that if an elderly person intends to make gifts and may want to use the Medicaid program to help pay for care, then prior to the gifting, the elderly person or his/her family should consult with a certified elder law attorney.

How can I learn the details about the Medicaid program? When asking a legal question about the Medicaid program or any other legal issue, it is imperative that a person obtain advice from a competent attorney. A person not licensed to practice law in Texas commits an offense if the person charges a fee for representing or aiding an applicant or recipient in procuring assistance from the Department of Social Services. A person commits an offense if the person advertises, holds himself or herself out for, or solicits the procurement of assistance from the department. An offense under this section is a Class A misdemeanor.

If the transfer rules remain, I have no problem with transferring assets to my kids, and putting it all in their names, and letting the three years go by, so that they own it. What's wrong with that? First of all, there's an ethical issue in trying to hide your money that way. We talked about that earlier. Secondly, there's a very practical issue. Your kids may be stable now, but what about four, five, or six years from now, and what if they get sued and all your money's taken? What if they marry somebody who turns out to be irresponsible, and that person is sued? When you transfer ownership of your money or property to your kids, that's irrevocable.

What about transferring moneys to a charity through an irrevocable trust? That's very noble. Again, just because it's an irrevocable trust, doesn't, in this case, mean the State cannot come back and seize it. If it is still within the three- to five-year period, depending upon the recipient, the State can say, "Hey, tough, that money was legally yours. If you transferred it out, you are responsible for coming up with that money to pay for your first several months or first several years of Medicaid."

Medicaid Documents/Eligibility

Common Medicaid Mistakes and Misconceptions

Even with the most noble and honest intentions, it's still possible to make mistakes on a Medicaid application. This is particularly true if you have a misconceived notion in your mind as to what Medicaid is for, what you are entitled to, and what you can get away with just because you feel it's owed to you. Here are the most common mistakes and misconceptions about Medicaid.

- Transferring assets without taking into account the transfer rules and penalties.
- Confusing the look-back period and the transfer penalty period.
- Making transfers without the proper authority.
- Relying on outdated or poorly drafted durable powers of attorney (or other estate planning documents).
- Neglecting to disclose all known income, assets, or gifts, or neglecting to inform Medicaid of the receipt of new or additional income or assets or gifts in the future.

- Failing to include the gross income of an applicant when applying for benefits.
- Improperly establishing a qualified income trust (called a "QIT" or "Miller trust"), or failing to maintain the Miller trust as required by Medicaid.
- Failing to determine whether or not the nursing home accepts Medicaid payments.
- Believing that Medicare pays for long-term nursing home costs.
- Making transfers into, or out of, the wrong type(s) of trusts.
- Thinking that the $11,000 annual gift tax exclusion limits Medicaid planning. The gift tax exclusion does *not* limit Medicaid gifts to that amount.
- Selling an exempt resource, such as the home, after Medicaid qualification.
- When using a monthly gift strategy, failing to limit the total of all gifts in a given month to the recommended amount. (This includes failing to take other gifts, such as religious donations, into account.)
- Failing to make a pre-need burial arrangement an *irrevocable* agreement.
- Not making certain that the applicant is in a Medicaid bed at the time of application.
- Making a series of large gifts and applying for Medicaid before the penalty period has expired for the *last* gift in the series.
- Failing to take into account the potential seizures of the client's home for estate recovery.
- Overlooking the potential need to arrange for Medicaid arrangement for *both* spouses (i.e., assisted living vs. hospice vs. chronic care, etc.).

CHAPTER SUMMARY

If you took nothing else away from this chapter, remember this: Medicaid is *not* the answer! It is not a long-term care alternative that should be entered into lightly because there is no automatic qualification, and you stand to lose all the assets you accumulated over your lifetime, including your home. You will lose them real fast and potentially be fined if you choose to defraud Uncle Sam to get on Medicaid.

On the other hand, if you have no other alternatives, if your finances are spent, *do* apply for Medicaid—if and only if this is truly your last alternative. Otherwise, you're cheating yourself, your loved one, and some other unfortunate individual who's rightfully entitled to the Medicaid bed or funds you or your loved one are using simply because you decided to outsmart the government.

ACTION STEPS

- ❑ Vow to yourself that you will plan *not* to be on Medicaid; Medicaid will not be your first option for long-term care.
- ❑ Ignore your know-it-all friends and seek professional advice about applying for Medicaid.
- ❑ Be honest with yourself about why you're applying for Medicaid: If you don't truly need it, leave it for someone who does.

CONCLUSION

The greatest disadvantage to government assistance is that the government takes control and they get to decide when, where, and how you or your loved one will receive care. I can think of no

other incentive more compelling to motivate you to *plan ahead.*
That, my friend, is the entire premise of this book. Only by planning ahead and becoming proactive about your future long-term
care needs will you avoid the need for Medicaid.

A well-laid-out plan puts financial and medical decisions where
they belong: *in your hands.*

Medicaid at a Glance*

For the Applicant

Maximum Allowable Monthly Income	$1,735
Maximum Allowable Countable Resources	$2,000

For the Community Spouse

Maximum Allowable Monthly Income   No Maximum

Protected Monthly Income for the Community Spouse is the greatest of:

a) 100% of the Community Spouse's personal income, or

b) up to $2,377.50 of the couple's combined income

Maximum Allowable Countable Resources:

P.R.A. = **P**rotected **R**esource **A**mount for the community spouse is one-half of the couple's countable resources with a Maximum of $95,100 (Minimum is $19,020).

The P.R.A. is based on the resources of the couple as of the first day of the month in which an applicant enters a Title XIX nursing facility.

---

*Subject to change, whenever Congress feels like it.

(Continues)

Medicaid at a Glance *(Continued)*

Transfer Penalties and Look-Back Periods

Penalties are assessed for uncompensated transfers, i.e. gifts or sales of resources for less than market value. The Medicaid benefit penalty for these types of transfers is:

1 month of Medicaid ineligibility for each transfer of $2,908 (for example, a transfer of $30,000 = an 11-month penalty)

Please note that the penalty periods begin the month of the transfer. Further, since August 1993, transfers have no maximum penalty period.

Look-Back Period is the time frame that can be examined prior to the date of application for Medicaid benefits. This examination is to assess financial data to verify assets and income—and also to determine if there were any uncompensated transfers that should be considered. The current Look-Back Period is 36 months.

Trusts and Other Legal Documents

Miller Trusts are suited for individuals who have a monthly income that exceeds the maximum of $1,735, but who would otherwise qualify for Medicaid. This trust is a Qualified Irrevocable Income Trust with specific Medicaid purposes.

Revocable Living Trusts are trusts established for estate planning reasons such as probate avoidance, estate settlement reduction, and ease of property distribution at death. Living Trusts do not generally create uncompensated transfers because the applicant maintains control of his or her assets as Trustee.

Advance Directives such as Durable Powers of Attorney, Health Care Powers of Attorney, and Directives to Physicians (Living Wills) are created to give another individual the ability to act on your behalf and in your best interest in the event of your incapacity, either physical or mental; by granting these powers with an advance directive, more costly and time consuming legal proceedings such as guardianship hearings can be avoided.

Table 5.1
Federal Estate Tax (Death Tax)

Calendar Year	Exemption	Highest Rate
2002	$1 million	50%
2003	$1 million	49%
2004	$1.5 million	48%
2005	$1.5 million	47%
2006	$2 million	46%
2007	$2 million	45%
2008	$2 million	45%
2009	$3.5 million	45%
2010	repealed	0%
2011	$1 million	55%

CHAPTER 6

The Power: How to
Stay Alive and Active

*We are now entering a generation who very likely will spend more
time taking care of elderly parents than we spent taking care of our
own children.*

—Senator Kit Bond

THIS CHAPTER IS DEDICATED SOLELY TO THE CAREGIVER, REGARDLESS
of whether this was a role you were forced into or one you volunteered for. It is designed to equip you with valuable information
as you step into or continue your caregiving role—a crash course,
if you will.

Just like child-rearing, caring for an elder adult is a full-time
job. And the truth of the matter is that many more American
adults have taken on this full-time responsibility, along with their
current occupations in the work force.

You may think that this is a chapter that doesn't apply to you
because, frankly, you're not a caregiver. You are healthy and so is
your immediate family. No worries there. Well, what happens if
tomorrow, Husband gets up from the couch and clutches his left
arm, writhing in pain? Or what if Sister or Brother calls you from

the hospital because Mom has had multiple strokes that have left one side of her body paralyzed? I've said this before and I'll say it again: The point of this book is to *prevent* the inevitable. We don't know what will happen tomorrow, but if we prepare today, we'll be that much better off. So read on!

According to a recent study by the American Association for Retired Persons (AARP), 44.4 million of us provide unpaid care to another adult. What's more 6 out of 10 are either working or have worked while providing care for that adult. Of that number 62 percent had to make some type of adjustment to their work life, whether it was going in at a later time or cutting down the number of hours. Some even quit their jobs altogether.

If you're a guy you might say, *But, Doc, I don't have to worry about that! Most caregivers are female.* Guess again. That same study conducted by the AARP found that increasingly, many caregivers are *men*. So, whether you're a man or a woman, this could be a very harsh reality for you.

Facts:

- More than 80 percent of caregivers say they assist relatives.
- The average age of individuals between the ages of 18 and 49 who need care is 33 years.
- The average age of individuals over the age of 50 who need care is 75 years.
- Among the caregivers who are caring for someone other than their husband or wife, the most burdened caregivers say they make an average monthly financial contribution of $437 to the care of that person.
- Almost one in five (17 percent) caregivers say they provide 40 or more hours of care per week.

Maybe you're beyond the "what if" stage. You're right smack in the middle of it. The need to care for your loved one is staring you in the face. What are you going to do? Will you choose a nursing home or just hire someone to care for your loved one? Or will you choose to shoulder the brunt of that awesome responsibility? There is no right or wrong answer, but this chapter focuses on those who choose to care for their loved ones at home.

Whatever the reason, you didn't choose a home health-care provider or a nursing home bed for your loved one. You chose to take care of your loved one yourself. He or she may be permanently injured or terminally ill. And you're now the cook, nurse, babysitter, psychologist, and activities director all rolled into one. How will you wear all these hats and still manage to stay alert and alive, healthy and happy? After all, it's a 24-7 job.

Perhaps you've been a caregiver for several years. Maybe you're just starting out. Maybe you have questions swimming in your head:

- "Why me?"
- "Why did she/he have to" (take your pick): "have a stroke," "have that accident," "eat fatty foods all the time," "forget to take his medicine," "forget to wear a seat belt?"
- "Why doesn't anyone help me?"
- "How long can I last?"
- "What will happen to him if something happens to me?"
- "It wasn't supposed to end this way; we just started our retirement!"

No matter how much you love your spouse or parent—and whether you chose to care for him or her or not—you will at times feel: hopeless, exhausted, frustrated, resentful, humiliated, angry, guilty, overwhelmed, and confused.

To make matters worse, people don't seem to be very sensitive to your feelings. They may say things like:

- "It's okay, honey, it's just your cross to bear."
- "If you had gotten long-term care a long time ago, this wouldn't be happening."
- "You must have done something wrong to be punished this way."
- "Throw him/her on Medicaid. Let the government take care of him/her."
- "Just let him/her die."
- "He/She is not worth it; you have your own life to live."

Attitude

In spite of the mixed emotions and the judgmental and critical comments from those around you, you are committed to be the one to care for your loved one. You *love them,* and *you value life.* Good for you!

You're tough. You've got tough love. And you're going to care for your loved one. Indeed, that's the first step: *commitment.* The second is: *reality.* The third step is realizing that what you've got and where you are is plenty good enough to build again. I encourage you to repeat these words aloud. Allow these words to stick to your subconscious. *What you've got and where you are is plenty good enough to build again.*

I encourage you to practice the attitudes I talk about in Doc's Medicine for Life, in Chapter 3, under the section "Emotional Health." These are the attitudes that will empower you to be a victorious caregiver. See your loved one as your patient.

You may say *Doc, that sounds so clinical and cold.* Clinical, yes;

cold, no. It's important that you objectify yourself so that you can see your loved one as your patient. The truth of the matter is that this is not:

- The man/woman you married.
- The child you reared.
- The parent you obeyed.

This is your *patient* and you need to exercise loving control, whether you feel like it or not and whether they understand it or not.

As a caregiver, it's important that you get real with your emotions. Frustration is a natural emotion that arises from caring for another individual. There's nothing wrong with it! It only becomes wrong when you act on that frustration and cause harm to yourself or your loved one.

According to the Family Caregiver Alliance, it's extremely important to recognize what *is* and what is *not* in your power to change—how very true! Trying to change uncontrollable or, better yet, *unchangeable* situations gives rise to frustration. There's a popular prayer that's often sold in various gift stores on plaques and mugs. Perhaps you're familiar with it. It says:

> God, grant me the serenity to accept the things I cannot change, courage to change the things I can, and the wisdom to know the difference.

If you're a caregiver, I encourage you to post this in several places throughout your home—on your forehead if you have to. There is no other situation where this can be more applicable.

If your loved one is paralyzed, you can't control how much time it takes you to bathe, dress, or feed him or her. What you can control is your attitude toward the activity. That is within your control. Getting angry or frustrated won't get you anywhere.

Something else you will find helpful is knowing yourself. Huh, you say? Well, if you know yourself, you can know early on if your blood's starting to boil. Maybe you're caring for your loved one *and* holding a full-time job. Maybe Hotshot Boss wasn't so kind or understanding today when you showed up five minutes late because you were waiting for the aide to show up. So, he's made your day miserable, and now it's the end of your workday—outside of the home, that is—and it's time for you to pick up where you left off with Mom or Dad (or husband or wife).

If you're feeling anger from another situation, give yourself time to cool off. *Don't* take it out on your loved one. They can't help but be helpless. How do you think they feel knowing they have to depend on you? How much worse would it make them feel to know that you resent them for it?

So before you do something you may regret, call the aide or friend before you leave work, tell them what's going on, and ask them to give you five or so minutes to take a brisk walk. You'll be glad you did.

Actions

What else should you do besides adjust your attitude? Here are some ideas:

- *Talk to yourself.* If you recall from Chapter 4, the most important conversation you have, besides prayer, is the one you have with yourself every day. Remember what we learned: What if you lived with somebody who constantly said to you, *You're stupid. You never do anything right. I can't believe you missed that opportunity. Nothing ever goes right for you.* We agreed that neither of us would live with such a demeaning person. Well, that's the person you become when you talk to yourself in that manner.

Often, we talk to ourselves in ways that we would never talk to anyone else. And we certainly wouldn't allow anyone else to talk to us like that, either. So remember to talk to yourself in positive, affirmative ways. *I can do this. I learned a lot from this; I'll do it better next time.*

- *Talk to your physician.* Find a physician who is supportive of your efforts. Find one who will partner with you and help you get through this caregiving challenge.
- *Talk to your family, friends, and neighbors.* Let them know that you need a night out. Let them know that you need someone to babysit your loved one periodically. It is a sign of strength to ask for help. Earlier, I pointed out that most caregivers die before the care receiver, and one of the reasons is that they refuse to ask for help.
- *Talk to your local church.* If you don't have any close neighbors or friends in your community, call local churches. You do not have to be a member of that church. Churches are always looking for opportunities to reach out and provide voluntary support.
- *Talk to your loved one in terms of "I" not "you."* In other words, don't say, "You shouldn't have locked that bathroom door—that was bad," or "You shouldn't have knocked over your cereal bowl," or "You shouldn't have gotten up so early." Remember that, when we age, we display more childlike tendencies because we can no longer care for ourselves.

Your loved one is now a child—a confused, fragile child. Instead of saying "You did this" or "You did that," you say,

"Next time, I will help you in the bathroom, so that doesn't happen again." "Next time, I'll put something under the cereal bowl, so it doesn't spill." It does you no good to pile on guilt, attacks, and defensiveness on your patient. It just builds frustration within you.

- *Talk to God.* It's practical and therapeutic. Studies have documented that prayer works. It works in practical results. It works in personal relief. By providing a sense of serenity, it can actually lower blood pressure and overall stress.

- *Laugh.* There's a reason why it's been dubbed the "best medicine." Instead of getting yourself worked up over a mistake you made, learn to laugh it off. You will find that your days will go much smoother if you do.

- *Write to yourself.* Keep a daily journal. When I was a marriage and family counselor, I insisted that my clients write a journal of what was going on in their heads and in their hearts. There is something therapeutic about getting it all out on paper. When you write it down, it dramatizes that you have control of the problems; the problems do not have control over you.

- *Write down personal goals.* Give yourself something to live for and strive for beyond caring for your loved one. Whether it's 15 minutes to an hour, dedicate some time *every day* to your personal goal, no matter how tired you are. It's important that you have something to look forward to so that your days don't become monotonous or dreary.

   For example, I am a marathon runner. When I round the corner on my last 200 yards and I see the finish line in the distance, that keeps me going. My legs feel like concrete, my lungs are on fire, my body is soaked in hot, sticky sweat. I know I can't take another step, but there it is, the goal. I see it; I know it's there. When I see a goal and I know I am making progress toward it, that's what fuels me to keep going.

- *Claim solutions.* With God, there is always a solution. Faith in the future provides power in the present. Write down whatever the specific challenge is in caring for your loved one. Write down a variety of solutions. They don't have to be perfect, exact, or practical. But write them down. Then go back and choose the two or three that will work.

- *Exercise.* Get someone to babysit and go out every evening or every morning and take that 30-minute walk. Put a couple of chairs together at your house and do some pull-ups or push-ups on them. Do jumping jacks in your living room. This is survival for you. This is survival for your loved one.

- Last, but certainly not least:
  - Eat healthy.
  - Don't use food as an escape.
  - Take a nap. Put your loved one down for a nap at the same time.
  - Get a good night's rest *every* night.
  - Get out. Use an adult day care center or a paid babysitter to get out. Socialize, dance, go to church, get out, and get relaxed and refreshed.

Caring for your loved one is a huge responsibility, but not impossible. You can do it! No one said it would be easy, but know that you're not alone. Here's a very telling article about the state of elder care today. The information is so invaluable that I felt it was imperative for the entire article to be included in this book.

Compassion in Action, One Woman's Story[1]

*An almost clichéd form of Christian service
to the elderly remains one of the most vital.*

Virginia Stem Owens

When the care of my parents fell to me six years ago, I knew I would need help if they were to stay in their own home. I beat the bushes for reliable helpers who could provide personal care for my mother, do light housework, and sometimes cook my parents a hot meal at noon. After learning that home health care is not covered by Medicare, I looked at my parents' combined retirement income and saw that it could easily cover four hours of daily care.

Many members of my church, I discovered, were also caring for elderly parents. I asked them for referrals to possible helpers. Those leads proved few and unfruitful. The women already had more clients than they could handle.

Next, I checked into home health care agencies. Their services were limited to bathing, feeding, and setting up medications. They didn't do windows—or even clean bathrooms or cook meals. Also, they were shorthanded and could not guarantee what time of day or even what days their workers would be available. A regular routine was essential for my mother who, along with Parkinson's disease, suffered from stroke-related dementia.

At last, I found a new agency in town that provided senior services, including housework and cooking. Their hourly rate was reasonable. But we never knew who would show up. Some days it was Gloria, some days Sharice, and some days a person we'd never see again. The constant change of faces in her house didn't help my mother's growing paranoia.

Then we struck gold. Ella was willing and could cook. She was gentle with my mother, who quickly came to trust her. She listened attentively to my mother's ramblings as she bathed and dressed her. But, like many of the women who do this work, Ella was no spring chicken herself. After Christmas, she was diagnosed with cancer. By Easter, Ella was dead.

For some time my mother had been suffering small strokes. Then the big one hit. After three weeks in the hospital, she still needed round-the-clock nursing care. Thus began our introduction to Fair Acres, the best of three local nursing homes. At that point, I thought my mother could not survive a year in her condition. I was wrong. She lived at Fair Acres almost five years.

Christian media and education about family life have focused primarily on child-rearing. Little attention has been given to caring for aging parents. In that arena, Christians, like their unchurched neighbors, generally find themselves at a loss. Many Christians are wrestling with the question of how to incorporate the commandment to honor their fathers and mothers in their already crowded lives.

A quick survey of the history and current status of nursing homes may help us think more seriously and concretely about the continuing, pressing need to honor the elderly in one of the tried and truest ways.

How Did This Happen?

How elderly Americans have been cared for has changed markedly over the centuries. The colonialists duplicated the English Poor Laws system, which obliged church parishes to maintain the infirm and destitute within their precincts. Of course, most parents were cared for by their families. But, if you were old, poor, and childless during the early years of this country, chances are you went to a workhouse or poor farm.

Residents were often kept under lock and key and had to wear uniforms in the hope that public humiliation would keep down their numbers. These establishments were a catchall not only for the elderly, but also for the "deaf, dumb, blind, idiots, aged and sick, poor children, unfortunate women, insane."

Owing to the country's new Constitution, however, the responsibility of funding public poorhouses passed from church to state. Some states solved the problem simply by boarding their elderly in private homes in order to save the expense of building and maintaining a facility. Tennessee auctioned off its paupers to farmers looking for cheap labor. New Jersey law forbade the emancipation of slaves over the age of 40 for fear the state would have to support them in their declining years.

Caring for old people—which many of *Christianity Today's* readers are or will soon be doing—will be one of the major challenges to the nation in the next decade. We now live longer, albeit with many diseases and disabilities we never survived to experience before. Babies born in 2000 can now expect to live to the age of 73—23 more years than the 1910 crop of babies.

No One at Home Anymore

A 2002 study by the research agency Zogby International measured the differences in expectations between parents 65 and older still living in their homes and their adult children. About half of the children believed their parents would want to live with them as they aged. But two-thirds of the parents did not want to live with their children.

Almost all the children expected to personally care for

their parents' daily needs at some point. But how realistic is this? Relatively few adult children, Christian or otherwise, now live near their parents. Also, in most middle-aged marriages, both people work outside the home. Their children may be in daycare or school during the day, but no one is home to look after an aging, infirm parent.

In "The Death of the Hired Man," Robert Frost defines home as "the place where, when you have to go there, they have to take you in."[2] But no longer. In fact, if you went there, chances are you'd find nobody home.

Most of my mother's fellow nursing home residents would call themselves Christian, as would a majority of their children. Some local churches hold regular services or Bible studies at Fair Acres. But few churches in this country actually own or operate nursing homes. Those few generally cater to retired clergy, and their cost puts them beyond the reach of many members.

For 91 percent of American retirees, their Social Security check is their major source of income, hardly enough to cover nursing home costs. Indeed, if you're over 75 and live alone, chances are better than 50-50 that you live on less than $10,000 a year. Therefore, it should come as no surprise that 68 percent of all nursing home beds are paid for by Medicaid, with Medicare picking up another 8 percent.

When the Zogby poll asked about the cost of long-term care, only a third of the parents thought they would need their children's financial help. More of the children—44 percent—expected to shoulder some of those expenses.

But another look at the numbers opens a new problem more urgent than who pays the nursing home bill. I was shocked to learn that 46 percent of nursing home residents have no living children, and more than half have no close living relative.

Once a citizen of the nursing home nation, you no longer operate on a money economy. At Fair Acres the rich are those who can get to the dining room under their own steam, use the toilet by themselves, and can still speak and be understood. My mother arrived there with little of that capital.

Nevertheless, her fellow residents envied her wealth of daily family visits. My father never flagged in his faithfulness. During the five years my mother lived at Fair Acres, he missed spending mornings with her only about a dozen times, most during illnesses of his own. I relieved him in the afternoon. My mother's cousin also visited her twice a week, and a busy sister-in-law often came on Thursdays.

To Visit Widows and Orphans

Only a handful of residents enjoy such consistent companionship. Many have survived all their friends and family. If they have children, they likely live at some distance. The sad fact is that two-thirds of all nursing home residents have no regular visitors at all.

Most people visit nursing homes reluctantly. The whiffs of urine that inevitably pervade such facilities, the monotonous cries for help, the faces frozen with despair or dementia can unsettle one's own psyche. We can't help wondering, Will that be me? Will I end up in a place like this? As the gap between your age and that of the average nursing home resident narrows, the question becomes persistent.

Christians with aging parents might ponder Jesus' provision for his mother, made in his own last extremity. "Behold, thy mother!" he tells his beloved disciple. "And from that hour that disciple took her into his own home." Money isn't mentioned, only the relationship.

Prudent financial planning is necessary, but money will not keep the body from wearing out. Nor can dollars defend against isolation and loneliness. Fair Acres' residents value above all companionship—someone to listen to their stories and tell them what's happening in the outside world. When you can't talk, you still want someone to hold your hand, watch the sun set or the rain fall, share a cookie, hum a tune, remember your birthday, hand you a Kleenex for your tears.

Relationships, even more than pension funds, require care and cultivation. Jesus taught that our heart and our treasure are found in the same location. Add value to your relationships every year, like an IRA contribution. Reach out to other people. Express gratitude to friends and family. And, even if it's hard, visit someone in a nursing home.

Virginia Stem Owens is a writer living in Huntsville, Texas. Her most recent book, which she wrote with her husband David, is Living Next Door to the Death House *(Eerdmans, 2003).*

This telling article brings us to my next point: How can I help? If you're not caring for an elderly parent or spouse, but you know someone who is, you don't have to stand idly by. *But Doc, they don't need my help! They can get along just fine without me!* Are you willing to bet your life on it?

Richard Cory
By Edwin Arlington Robinson

Whenever Richard Cory went down town,
We people on the pavement looked at him:
He was a gentleman from sole to crown,
Lean favored, and imperially slim.

And he was always quietly arrayed,
And he was always human when he talked;
But still he fluttered pulses when he said,
"Good-morning" and he glittered when he walked.

And he was rich—yes, richer than a king—
And admirably schooled in every grace;
In time we thought that he was everything
To make us wish that we were in his place.

So on we worked, and waited for the light,
And went without the meat, and cursed the bread;
And Richard Cory, one calm summer night,
Went home and put a bullet through his head.[3]

The truth of the matter is that a person could be in a world of anguish and you wouldn't know it. Like lava, hot and violent, percolating below the crust, we all have problems, worries, and crises, ready to explode.

The normal human condition is that we are either: in a crisis, just coming out of a crisis, or going into a crisis.

In contrast to the normal American conversation, which is:

"How are you?"
"I'm fine, how about yourself?"
"Couldn't be better."
"No problems."

It's a show. Seldom do we acknowledge the hot, bubbly lava of distress. Caregivers especially don't talk about all their stress.

How do you help the caregiver? Let me count the thousands of ways.

- Shine their shoes.
- Change the oil in their car.
- Cook/bring them dinner.
- Do laundry.
- Babysit for an hour.

- Babysit for a weekend.
- Read aloud to the patient.
- Hug/kiss them often.
- Tell them jokes.
- Show them photos.
- Play games.
- Pray for them.
- Give them a back rub.

And the list goes on and on. The bottom line is that no matter what you do for them, whether big or small, they will appreciate it immensely. Sometimes, just knowing that someone else cares and is thinking of you makes all the difference in the world.

CHAPTER SUMMARY

So what did we learn? We learned that caring for a loved one is a reality facing many working adults today. We also learned that the likelihood that this could happen to you is high. We went through ways in which you can care for yourself and your loved one. We also learned how we in the community could become involved and lend a hand to the caregiver, finding ways to lighten the load.

ACTION STEPS

❑ Ask for help when you feel overwhelmed. Admit that no matter how vibrant you think you are, you can't do it all by yourself.
❑ If you're having a terrible day, don't take your emotions out on your loved one. Defuse your anger and your hostility before unleashing it on them.

❑ Make it a point to help out your neighbor at least once a week, if you know they're caring for an elder adult. Remember, every little bit you can do will go a long way!

❑ Before you care for your loved one, care for yourself: emotionally, mentally, physically, and spiritually!

CONCLUSION

I can't stress enough how important it is to plan, plan, and plan some more! This is the cure-all for any situation you may find yourself in. Careful planning is the only way to prevent disaster: in your health, your finances, your life. Planning *is* prevention.

That is the safety net that will stave off the pain and the plea of poor nursing home care and the denials and delays of government care. The right plan can help you to learn to live to 98 and love every moment as well as protect your profits and your peace of mind. Otherwise, you'll find yourself under the tormenting pressure that comes when it's too late to plan. Plan, plan, plan ahead (write it down!) so that your assets and legacy are left to your children or your favorite charity like you wished.

If you need additional assistance, you may write me at:

P.O. Box 814514
Dallas, TX 75381

> Your friend,
> Doc

And most of all, plan ahead so that this very wish becomes your own:

> *I want my final days to be at home, in my own bed or chair, with my wonderful family around me.*
>
> —Dr. Norman Vincent Peale

State Medicaid Offices

ALABAMA
Alabama Medicaid Agency
2500 Fairlane Drive
Montgomery, AL 36130
(205) 277-2710

ALASKA
Division of Medical Assistance
Dept of Health & Social Services
P.O. Box H
Juneau, AK 99811
(907) 465-3355

ARIZONA
Arizona Health Care Cost
  Containment System (AHCCS)
801 East Jefferson
Phoenix, AZ 85034
(602) 244-3655

ARKANSAS
Arkansas Dept of Human
  Resources
Medicaid
P.O. Box 1437
Little Rock, AR 72203
(501) 682-8502

CALIFORNIA
Medical Care Services
Dept of Health Services
714 P Street, Room 1253
Sacramento, CA 95814
(916) 332-5824

COLORADO
Colorado Dept of Social Services
Health & Medical Services
1575 Sherman Street, 10th Floor
Denver, CO 80203
(303) 866-5901

CONNECTICUT
Dept of Income Maintenance
110 Bartholomew Avenue
Hartford, CT 06106
(203) 566-2008

DELAWARE
Division of Social Services
Dept of Health & Social Services
Medicaid
P.O. Box 906
1901 N. Dupont Highway
Briggs Building
New Castle, DE 19720
(302) 421-6140

DISTRICT OF COLUMBIA
Office of Health Care Financing
DC Dept of Human Services
2100 Martin Luther King, Jr
   Avenue SE
Suite 302
Washington DC 20020
(202) 727-0735

FLORIDA
Medicaid Provider/Consumer
   Relations
1317 Winewood Boulevard
Building 6, Room 260
Tallahassee, FL 32399
(904) 488-8291

GEORGIA
Georgia Dept of Medical
   Assistance
2 Martin Luther King, Jr Drive
1220-C West Tower
Atlanta, GA 30334

HAWAII
Health Care Administration
Dept of Human Services
P.O. Box 339
Honolulu, HI 96809
(808) 586-5392

IDAHO
Bureau of Welfare Medical
   Programs
Dept of Health & Welfare
450 W. State Street
Boise, ID 83720
(208) 334-5747

ILLINOIS
Division of Medical Programs
Illinois Dept of Public Aid
201 S. Grand Avenue East
Springfield, IL 62743
(217) 782-2570

INDIANA
Indiana State Dept of Public
   Welfare
100 N. Senate Avenue
State Office Building, Rm 701
Indianapolis, IN 46204
(317) 232-6865

IOWA
Division of Medical Services
Dept of Human Services
Hoover State Office Building
Des Moines, IA 50319
(515) 281-8621

KANSAS
Dept of Social & Rehabilitative
    Services
Division of Medical Services
1915 Harrison Street
Docking State Office Building
Room 628-S
Topeka, KS 66612
(913) 296-3981

KENTUCKY
Dept of Medicaid Services
275 E. Main Street, 3rd Floor
Frankfort, KY 40621
(502) 564-4321

LOUISIANA
Bureau of Health Services
    Financing
P.O. Box 91031
Baton Rouge, LA 70821
(504) 342-3956

MAINE
Dept of Human Services
Bureau of Income Maintenance
State House Station #11
Whitten Road
Augusta, ME 04333
(207) 289-5088

MARYLAND
Medical Care Policy
    Administration
201 W. Preston Street
Baltimore, MD 21201
(301) 225-1432

MASSACHUSETTS
Division of Medical Assistance
650 Washington Street
Boston, MA 02111
(617) 348-5500

MICHIGAN
Medical Services
    Administration
Dept of Social Services
P.O. Box 30037
Lansing, MI 48909
(517) 335-5000

MINNESOTA
Dept of Human Services
Health Care Programs Division
444 Lafayette Road
St. Paul, MN 55155
(612) 296-8517

MISSISSIPPI
Division of Medicaid
801 Robert E. Lee Building
239 N. Lamar Street
Jackson, MS 39201
(601) 359-6050

MISSOURI
Division of Medical Services
Dept of Social Services
P.O. Box 6500
Jefferson City, MO 65102
(314) 751-3425

MONTANA
Medicaid Services Division
Dept of Social & Rehabilitation
   Services
111 Sanders Street
P.O. Box 4210
Helena, MT 59604
(406) 444-4540

NEBRASKA
Nebraska Dept of Social Services
301 Centennial Mall South
P.O. Box 95026
Lincoln, NE 68509
(402) 471-3121

NEVADA
Division of Welfare
Dept of Human Resources
2527 N. Carson Street
Carson City, NV 89710
(702) 687-4378

NEW HAMPSHIRE
Division of Human Services
Office of Medical Services
6 Hazen Drive
Concord, NH 03301
(603) 271-4344

NEW JERSEY
Division of Medical Assistance &
   Health Services
Dept of Human Services
CN-712
7 Quakerbridge Plaza
Trenton, NJ 08625
(609) 588-2600

NEW MEXICO
Medical Assistance Division
Dept of Human Services
P.O. Box 2348
Santa Fe, NM 87504
(505) 827-4315

NEW YORK
Division of Medical Assistance
New York State Dept of Social
   Services
40 N. Pearl Street
Albany, NY 12243
(518) 474-9132

NORTH CAROLINA
Division of Medical Assistance
Dept of Human Resources
1985 Umstead Drive
P.O. Box 29529
Raleigh, NC 27626
(919) 733-2060

NORTH DAKOTA
North Dakota Dept of Human
   Services
Medical Services
600 East Boulevard
Bismarck, ND 58505
(701) 224-2321

*NORTHERN MARIANA
   ISLANDS*
Dept of Community & Cultural
   Affairs
Office of the Governor
Saipan, CM 96950
(670) 332-9722

OHIO
Dept of Human Services
Medicaid Administration
30 E. Broad Street, 31st Floor
Columbus, OH 43266
(614) 644-0410

OKLAHOMA
Division of Medical Services
Dept of Human Services
P.O. Box 25352
Oklahoma City, OK 73125
(405) 557-2539

OREGON
Office of Medical Assistance
Dept of Human Resources
203 Public Service Building
Salem, OR 97310
(503) 378-2263

PENNSYLVANIA
Dept of Public Welfare
Health & Welfare Building
P.O. Box 2675
Harrisburg, PA 17120
(717) 787-3119

PUERTO RICO
Dept of Social Services
P.O. Box 11398
Santurce, PR 00910
(809) 722-7400

RHODE ISLAND
Dept of Human Services
600 New London Avenue
Cranston, RI 02920
(401) 464-3575

SOUTH CAROLINA
South Carolina Health &
    Human Services Finance
    Commission
1801 Main Street
Columbia, SC 29201
(803) 253-6128

SOUTH DAKOTA
Medical Services
Dept of Social Services
700 Governor's Drive
Kneip Building
Pierre, SD 57501
(605) 773-3495

TENNESSEE
Bureau of Medicaid
729 Church Street
Nashville, TN 37247
(615) 741-0213

TEXAS
Dept of Human Services
Health Care Services
P.O. Box 149030
Austin, TX 78714
(512) 450-3050

UTAH
Division of Health Care Financing
Utah Dept of Health
P.O. Box 16580
Salt Lake City, UT 84116
(801) 538-6151

VERMONT
Dept of Social Welfare
Vermont Agency of Human
   Services
103 S. Main Street
Waterbury, VT 05676
(802) 241-2880

VIRGINIA
Virginia Dept of Medical
   Assistance Services
600 E. Broad Street, Suite 1300
Richmond, VA 23212
(804) 786-7933

VIRGIN ISLANDS
Dept of Human Services
Barbel Plaza South
St. Thomas, VI 00802
(809) 774-0930

WASHINGTON
Medicaid Recipient Assistance &
   Information
617 8th Avenue SE
Olympia, WA 98504
1-800-562-3022

WEST VIRGINIA
Division of Medical Care
West Virginia Dept of Human
   Services
State Capital Complex
Building 6, Room 717B
Charleston, WV 25305
(304) 348-8990

WISCONSIN
Division of Health
Wisconsin Dept of Health &
   Social Services
P.O. Box 309
Madison, WI 53701
(608) 266-2522

WYOMING
Medical Assistance Services
Dept of Health & Social
   Services
6101 Yellowstone
Cheyenne, WY 82002
(307) 777-7531

APPENDIX B

State Insurance Commmissions

ALABAMA
Commissioner of Insurance
135 South Union Street #160
P.O. Box 303351
Montgomery, AL 36130-3351
(334) 241-4101

ALASKA
Director of Insurance
P.O. Box 110805
Juneau, AK 99811
(907) 465-2515

AMERICAN SAMOA
Office of the Governor
Pago Pago, AS 96796
(684) 633-4116

ARIZONA
Director of Insurance
2910 N. 44th Street
Suite 210
Phoenix, AZ 85018
(602) 912-8456

ARKANSAS
Insurance Commissioner
University Tower Building
1123 South University Avenue
Suite 400
Little Rock, AR 72204
(501) 686-2909

CALIFORNIA
Insurance Commissioner
45 Fremont Street, 23rd Floor
San Francisco, CA 94105
(415) 904-5410

COLORADO
Commissioner of Insurance
1560 Broadway, Suite 850
Denver, CO 80202
(303) 894-7499

CONNECTICUT
Insurance Commissioner
Insurance Department
165 Capitol Avenue
State Office Building, Room 425
P.O. Box 816
Hartford, CT 06142
(203) 297-3802

DELAWARE
Insurance Commission
Rodney Building
841 Silver Lake Boulevard
Dover, DE 19904
(302) 739-4251

DISTRICT OF COLUMBIA
Commissioner of Insurance
Department of Consumer and
   Regulatory Affairs
One Judiciary Square
441 4th Street, NW
8th Floor North
Washington, DC 20001
(202) 727-8000

FLORIDA
Insurance Commission
State Treasurer's Office
State Capitol
Plaza Level Eleven
Tallahassee, FL 32399-0300
(904) 922-3100

GEORGIA
Commissioner of Insurance
7th Floor, West Tower
Floyd Building
2 Martin Luther King, Jr Drive
Atlanta, GA 30334
(404) 656-2056

GUAM
P.O. Box 2796
855 West Marine Drive
Agana, GU 96910
011-671-477-1040

HAWAII
Insurance Commissioner
Department of Commerce and
   Consumer Affairs
P.O. Box 3614
Honolulu, HI 96811
(808) 586-2790

IDAHO
Director of Insurance
500 S. 10th Street
P.O. Box 83720
Boise, ID 83720
(208) 334-4250

ILLINOIS
Director of Insurance
State of Illinois
320 West Washington Street
4th Floor
Springfield, IL 62767
(217) 782-4515

INDIANA
Commissioner of Insurance
311 West Washington Street
Suite 300
Indianapolis, IN 46204-2787
(317) 232-3520

IOWA
Commissioner of Insurance
Lucas State Office Building
6th Floor
Des Moines, IA 50319
(515) 281-5523

KANSAS
Commissioner of Insurance
420 S.W. 9th Street
Topeka, KS 66612
(913) 296-3071

KENTUCKY
Insurance Commissioner
215 West Main Street
P.O. Box 517
Frankfort, KY 40602
(502) 564-6027

LOUISIANA
Commissioner of Insurance
950 N. 5th Street
P.O. Box 94214
Baton Rouge, LA 70804-9214
(504) 342-5423

MAINE
Superintendent of Insurance
State Office Building
State House, Station 34
Augusta, ME 04333
(207) 582-8707

MARYLAND
Insurance Commissioner
51 St. Paul Place (Stanbalt Bldg)
7th Floor-South
Baltimore, MD 21202
(410) 333-2521

MASSACHUSETTS
Commissioner of Insurance
470 Atlantic Avenue
Boston, MA 02210
(617) 521-7794

MICHIGAN
Insurance Commissioner
P.O. Box 30220
Lansing, MI 48909
611 West Ottawa Street
2nd Floor
North Lansing, MI 48933
(517) 373-9273

MINNESOTA
Commissioner of Commerce
133 East 7th Street
St Paul, MN 55101
(612) 296-6694

MISSISSIPPI
Commissioner of Insurance
1804 Walter Sillers Bld
P.O. Box 79
Jackson, MS 39205
(601) 359-3569

MISSOURI
Director, Department of
   Insurance
301 West High Street, 6 North
P.O. Box 690
Jefferson City, MO 65102-0690
(314) 751-4126

MONTANA
Commissioner of Insurance
126 North Sanders
Mitchell Building
Room 270
P.O. Box 4009
Helena, MT 59604
(406) 444-2040

NEBRASKA
Director of Insurance
Terminal Building
941 O Street, Suite 400
Lincoln, NE 68508
(402) 471-2201

NEVADA
Commissioner of Insurance
Capitol Complex
1685 Hot Springs Road, Suite 152
Carson City, NV 89710
(702) 687-4270

NEW HAMPSHIRE
Insurance Commissioner
169 Manchester Street
Concord, NH 03301
(603) 271-2261

NEW JERSEY
Commissioner of Insurance
20 West State Street
CN325
Trenton, NJ 08625
(609) 292-5350

NEW MEXICO
Superintendent of Insurance
Pera Bldg.
P.O. Drawer 1269
Santa Fe, NM 87504-1269
(505) 827-4500

NEW YORK
Superintendent of Insurance
160 West Broadway
New York, NY 10013
(212) 602-0429

NORTH CAROLINA
Commissioner of Insurance
430 North Salisbury Street
Dobbs Building
Raleigh, NC 27603
P.O. Box 26387
Raleigh, NC 27611
(919) 733-7349

NORTH DAKOTA
Commissioner of Insurance
Capitol Bldg., 600 East Boulevard
5th Floor
Bismarck, ND 58505
(701) 328-2440

OHIO
Director of Insurance
2100 Stella Court
Columbus, OH 43215
(614) 644-2651

OKLAHOMA
Insurance Commissioner
1901 North Walnut
Oklahoma City, OK 73105
P.O. Box 53408
Oklahoma City, OK 73152-3404
(405) 521-2828

OREGON
Insurance Commissioner
440 Labor & Industries Bldg
Salem, OR 97310
(503) 378-4100

PENNSYLVANIA
Insurance Commissioner
Strawberry Square
13th Floor
Harrisburg, PA 17120
(717) 783-0442

PUERTO RICO
Fernandez Juncos Station
P.O. Box 8330
Santurce, PR 00910
(809) 722-8686

RHODE ISLAND
Director of Business Regulation
  and Insurance Commissioner
State of Rhode Island
233 Richmond Street, Suite 233
Providence, RI 02903-4237
(401) 277-2223

SOUTH CAROLINA
Chief Insurance Commissioner
1612 Marion Street
Columbia, SC 29201
P.O. Box 100105
Columbia, SC 29202-3105
(803) 737-6160

SOUTH DAKOTA
Director of Insurance
Insurance Building
910 East Sioux Avenue
Pierre, SD 57501
(605) 773-3563

TENNESSEE
Commissioner of Commerce and
  Insurance
Volunteer Plaza
500 James Robertson Parkway
Nashville, TN 37243
(615) 741-2241

TEXAS
Commissioner of Insurance
333 Guadalupe Street
Austin, TX 78701-1998
(512) 463-6464

UTAH
Commissioner of Insurance
3110 State Office Building
Salt Lake City, UT 84114
(801) 538-3804

VERMONT
Commissioner of Banking,
    Insurance and Securities
89 Main Street, Drawer 20
Montpelier, VT 05602
(802) 828-3301

VIRGINIA
Commissioner of Insurance
Tyler Building
P.O. Box 1157
Richmond, VA 23209
(804) 371-9694

VIRGIN ISLANDS
Kongens Gade #18
St. Thomas, VI 00802
(809) 774-2991

WASHINGTON
Insurance Commissioner
Insurance Bilding, AQ21
P.O. Box 40255
Olympia, WA 98504
(360) 753-7301

WEST VIRGINIA
Insurance Commissioner
2019 Washington Street, East
Charleston, WV 25305
(304) 558-3354

WISCONSIN
Commissioner of Insurance
121 East Wilson Street
P.O. Box 7873
Madison, WI 53707
(608) 266-0102

WYOMING
Insurance Commissioner
Herschler Building
122 West 25th Street, 3 East
Cheyenne, WY 82002
(307) 777-7401

Notes

Introduction *From Welfare to Wealth: My Story*

1. Alan Farnham, *Forbes: Great Success Stories* Forbes, Inc., John Wiley and Sons, 2000, 4.
2. See "Letter to Workers" from Social Security Commissioner Jo Anne Barnhart. "Social Security may be short of cash by 2013. The combined programs (Social Security and Medicare) may be cash-short by 2010."
3. Pelzer, Dave. *Help Yourself.* New York: The Penguin Group, 2000.

Chapter 1 *The Pain and the Plea: Nursing Home Abuse*

1. We acknowledge that many nursing homes are safe and many nursing home workers are conscientious. These conscientious workers join me in condemning the abusive practices of the derelict and dangerous homes.
2. Reference to actual client cases is common throughout this book. Names, places, and dates have been altered to protect confidentiality.
3. For a comprehensive list of the effects of physical and chemical restraints, go to: http://www.docgallagher.com.
4. A detailed list of common scenarios and noticeable signs can be found at: http://www.docgallagher.com.

Chapter 2 *The Problem: Denials and Delays*

1. Reprinted with permission. Kristin Davis, *Kiplinger's Personal Finance*, vol. 58, Issue 11, November 1, 2004, pp. 80–84.
2. Check with your tax advisor on the status of these provisions.

Chapter 3   *The Prevention: How to Make It to 98 and Love and Live Every Minute*

1. *Time*, August 30, 2004, pp. 44–45.
2. Reprinted with permission, AVAS Music Publishing Co., Inc., New York, NY, © 1969.
3. *Time*, August 30, 2004, p. 23.

Chapter 4   *The Plan: Powerful Strategies That Protect Profits and Provide Peace of Mind*

1. "S&P 500" refers to the Standard & Poor's 500, a list of stock of the top 500 companies in the United States. "S&P 500" is a trademark of the McGraw-Hill Companies, Inc.
2. Past performance is no guarantee of future results.

Chapter 5   *The Pressure: When It's Too Late to Plan*

1. From Diana Conway, "Cheating Uncle Sam for Mom and Dad." *Newsweek*, vol. 141, Issue 4, January 27, 2003. Reprinted by permission.
2. Warner, Jan L. and Jan Collins. *Jewish World Review*, June 11, 2003.

Chapter 6   *The Power: How to Stay Alive and Active*

1. Copyright © 2004 *Christianity Today*. September 2004, vol. 48, no. 9, page 58.
2. Reprinted with permission, Dodd, Mead & Co., Inc., New York, NY. *North of Boston*, © 1977.
3. Reprinted with permission, The Macmillan Company, New York, NY, © 1937.

Index

About the Author

Dr. W. Neil Gallagher (Ph.D., Brown University) is a retired university professor and faculty member on Zig Ziglar's "Born to Win" seminars.

A native of New York City, he is the host of "The Money Doctor's Show" and author of four books and 17 popular and professional articles, including articles in *The Journal of Value Inquiry, Philosophy and Phenomenological Research, Tall Windows: National Library Literary Review, The Commission, R.I. College Alumni Review,* and *Born to Win* newsletter.

For his humanitarian service as a Peace Corps teacher and medic in leper colonies in Thailand, he received the Foreign Service Award from the government of Thailand and the Outstanding Young Men of America Award.

Via radio, television, seminars, and his private practice, he has for 20 years counseled millions on effective strategies for long-term care, retirement, financial, and estate planning.

He lives in the Dallas area with his wife of 40 years, Gail, and their two children, Scotty and Amber.

An avid runner, he has completed the New York City Marathon and is training for his first triathlon.